CAMPAIGN
JOURNAL 2008

CAMPAIGN
JOURNAL 2008

A Chronicle of Vision, Hope, and Glory

Carlos J. Rangel

Routledge
Taylor & Francis Group

LONDON AND NEW YORK

First published 2009 by Transaction Publishers

2 Park Square, Milton Park, Abingdon, Oxfordshire OX14 4RN
711 Third Avenue, New York, NY 10017

Routledge is an imprint of the Taylor & Francis Group, an informa business

First issued in paperback 2017

Copyright © 2009 Taylor & Francis

Library of Congress Catalog Number: 2009026179

Library of Congress Cataloging-in-Publication Data

Rangel, Carlos J.
  Campaign journal 2008 : a chronicle of vision, hope, and glory / Carlos J. Rangel.
      p. cm.
  Includes bibliographical references and index.
  ISBN 978-1-4128-1083-8 (alk. paper)
     1. Presidents--United States--Election--2008. 2. Political campaigns--United States--History--21st century. 3. United States--Politics and government--2001- I. Title.

JK5262008 .R37 2009
324.973'0931--dc22

                                                    2009026179

  ISBN 13: 978-1-4128-1083-8 (hbk)
  ISBN 13: 978-1-138-50787-6 (pbk)

To Esmeralda and Julia

"Man must be able to dare to think truthfully and to act accordingly without fear of losing his franchise to live."—Buckminster Fuller, 1969

Contents

Acknowledgements

Any project such as this saps time and energy from other endeavors, so I am especially grateful to my wife, Dr. Esmeralda Garbi, whose patience and support allowed me to finish what started as a simple exchange of ideas in discussion and banter. Her keen insight, judgments and revisions made this a much better work. I wish to also thank Dr. Irving Louis Horowitz, who from his first glance to the partial manuscript encouraged me to turn it into a complete product, which I delivered to him on January 19, 2009, the day before the inauguration. I also appreciate the efforts of the editorial, marketing, and administrative staff of Transaction Publishers for turning the draft I handed in into the book you have in your hands, in particular Laurence Mintz and Maureen Feldman. There are countless others among family, old and new friends that supported, encouraged or otherwise assisted and helped in the making of this book. To all of them, I give my heartfelt gratitude.

Carlos J. Rangel
May 2009, Coral Springs, FL

Introduction

When in February 2007 the junior senator from Illinois announced his intention to run for president of the United States of America, his announcement came in almost under the radar. With this early start, one of the most remarkable U.S. political campaign seasons got under way in earnest. It would be a campaign that transformed the way our own society sees itself. For the first time, an African American was seen as a viable candidate for president, a woman was the early favorite to win, and potentially the oldest president to be sworn in could be elected.

Over the course of just a few months from 2007 to 2008, the political passions of many were rekindled or fired up. Some of us remembered why we were enthralled about politics in the first place. My personal political experience had ranged from staffing polling places to social activism. The 2008 presidential campaign season as it unfolded motivated me to write down thoughts and observations, most of which I then forwarded as letters to friends, family members, newspaper editors, columnists, journalists, my U.S. Congress representatives, David Axelrod and AKP&D Media—Senator Barack Obama's political campaign headquarters—the DNC, *Meet the Press*, *Morning Joe*, Speaker Nancy Pelosi, and others. Sometimes I sent a rough, almost ranting draft of a quick reaction to a current event, which I later edited and refined as part of the chapters included in this book. At other times I thought and wrote at length on a topic and then sent excerpts, as relevance to discussion befitted, to interested parties. The content and specifics of each chapter is not changed, however, and it represents the exact sentiments and information that I had at the time in which the original letter or thoughts were circulated. The date, indicated within each chapter section, reflects that timing.

I received specific feedback from some people, including Chuck Todd, senators Bill Nelson (D-FL) and Mel Martinez (R-FL), and Rep. Ron Klein (D-FL), and encouragement from Beatrice Rangel, chief of staff of former president of Venezuela Carlos Andrés Pérez, and others for which I am grateful.

1

I am proud of America, of what it represents, and of its promise of social justice embedded in the Constitution. I am an ordinary citizen, a typically average modern American. Typical and average in the same way that no one is and everyone is. As an American born abroad, I have multicultural roots; I have lived in major cities and little towns across America and in foreign countries in Europe and Latin America. I graduated from a small-town public high school in upstate New York, but also went to private Catholic school in Latin America. I went to college in New York City; I studied abroad in Italy, graduated from business school in Venezuela, and attended graduate school in Los Angeles, California. I have lived and worked in several U.S. and Latin American cities. I am a modern America man, much like any other, with a deep love of country, and great expectations about its development. My thoughts, positive and negative, are framed from what I have seen in America and elsewhere.

I am troubled, as many are, by current trends allowing and fostering ignorance, poverty, and divisiveness in America. These trends seem driven by factors and players in the sole pursuit of self-interest. My economics background taught me that man's pursuit of self-interest is the driver of economic and social development, but it also taught me that greed, when taken to an extreme and left unrestrained, leads to inequality and devastation. I believe some economic revisionism may be in order at this time, given the current state of our nation—from the economy to the "culture wars."

The chapters that follow were motivated by the unique combination of events that occurred during the remarkable electoral year of 2008. Many issues made this electoral season an exceptional one: a truly diverse field of candidates; fighting two wars abroad; and being on the verge of the worst economic downturn since the Great Depression. These chapters describe thus, in chronological order, my personal journey through the presidential elections, starting in early March and ending in late December of 2008. The book opens with the Democratic primaries, and follows through with the campaign, the debates, and the presidential election. The topics range from key differences between candidates regarding character, values and their positions on current issues such as health care, unemployment, tax policy, trade and the economy, among others. Throughout the book, I include my own positions regarding the topics that framed the political standings of the presidential candidates. I also present opinions and suggestions regarding campaign strategy—in a way, a cathartic response that helped me cope with the anxieties generated by this electoral process. The wide range of topical essays discuss the "hot topics" of the 2008 election such as McCain's VP choice, Joe the Plumber, and the financial industry bailout, as well as other domestic and international topics that, although never a core of the electoral debates or the newscast electoral topic of the day (i.e., international trade, the war on drugs and its links to terrorism, the outside influences to U.S. policy, etc.) are so significant that they will shape the future of our nation under any presidency.

Of course, such a review of political, policy, and election topics could not be exhaustive in a book and a format such as this one. Major omissions include the Middle East, the wars in Iraq and Afghanistan, and all things Israeli, as well as immigration. These and other topics, sometimes superficially glanced throughout this journal, could each fill various tomes on their own. And they have.

1

The Democratic Primaries

In the aftermath of the disappointing results of "Super Tuesday" (February 5, 2008), by which time she had expected to clinch the Democratic nomination, Senator Hillary Clinton became more aggressive in her attacks against Senator Barack Obama. Old politics would have suggested counterattacks by Senator Obama but, in a sign of things to come, he in fact did not pursue the aggressive attack style of old politics. His style developed as punctilious, cerebrally playing by the rules laid out, and strategizing accordingly.[1] In the end, this was like throwing a slider strike to the Clinton campaign, which only too late realized that the rules of the game had changed. However, she ignored these new rules until it was too late. Between Super Tuesday and the meeting of the Democratic National Convention Rules Committee, I wrote the following notes, some perhaps a little more passionate than fair-minded, including allegations that were perhaps more campaign fodder than fact.

So, She Won the Battle but…. Did She Lose the War?

March 7, 2008

The way Senator Clinton won last Tuesday, March 4, in Texas and in Ohio brings back into the fray what New Democrats have been reacting against. Her campaign's strategy apparent view that all she needs to do to win is to get half of the support plus one—disregarding the alienation of the disenfranchised half minus one—returns to the political arena the divisiveness that often characterized former President Clinton and the current President Bush. In winning by attacking she may have started a cycle that could bring down the election for the Democrats. Her personal attacks go to the core of what a candidate is: a qualified office holder. Contradicting the way she acted and reacted during the most recent two debates in which she praised Senator Obama, she now constantly disqualifies his capabilities as a possible

5

President. These attacks may have the potential consequence of Senator Obama's attacking back.

In the quickly fed misinformation and sound bite news that many voters use as a basis for their decision, attacking back may be the unfortunate path that Senator Obama's campaign takes. Because of her trajectory and years in the limelight, many allegations and unfounded charges have been made against Senator Clinton. The laundry list of attacks may include questioning her values and judgment regarding her allegedly philandering husband, charges about the so-called "Travelgate" and her renting of bedrooms at the White House, not to mention land deals in Arkansas—and some dirt on international fundraising with the Chinese around the time of the trade deals with that country.[2]

If Senator Obama's campaign goes the nasty route, the Republicans will be very happy. Regardless of who is the candidate for the Democratic Party, the Republicans will benefit from either one of them being portrayed over an extended period of time as naïve, inexperienced, and unknown, or with so much dirty laundry that the stench will permeate well into the fall.

Senator Clinton wants it both ways, first suggesting that Senator Obama is not qualified to be president, and then not disqualifying him as a potential VP for her ticket. Which is it then? Is he qualified or is he not? And, who would really want to be the VP in a Clinton co-presidency? Ralph Nader may be right. He has stated that if the Democrats do not win—given the current state of the country and given the status of the Republican Party—they may have to close up shop come November.[3]

The Numbers Game

March 11, 2008

Governor Ed Rendell of Pennsylvania was a guest at *Meet the Press* on March 9 with the late Tim Russert. On that occasion, he ardently supported Clinton's electoral math (Rendell 2008). The numbers upon which the following is based were published online by CNN, MSNBC and FOX at the time. The numbers crunch game was also thrown a wrench on account of Florida and Michigan, which held primaries in January, disregarding the scheduling guidelines of the Democratic National Committee (Shear 2007; Nagourney 2007). Florida and Michigan were punished by the DNC for jumpstarting the primary schedule by not having their delegates count towards the total number required to nominate the Democratic presidential candidate.

Governor Rendell's assertion that caucuses are not democratic processes was at best incredibly dismissive and at worst extremely divisive. Disqualifying the massive turnouts that we have seen in these processes in order to suggest that Senator Obama's success in caucuses is undemocratic seems to be a way of attempting to change the rules after the results. Suggesting that "shift workers and disabled senior citizens"—supposedly Senator Clinton's core constituencies—are disenfranchised by the caucus process is disingenuous (Rendell 2008). Many of these constituencies have let their opinions be known and have influenced caucus attendees. Caucus voters represent—in this manner—not only themselves, but mini-constituencies. Union leaders typically are caucus attendees, for example.

Arguably, primary early voting and mail-in ballots have resulted in political setbacks for Senator Obama because in every primary in which he has campaigned he has closed the gap as Election Day draws closer. Thus, it could be rendered as "undemocratic" that voters chose before actually knowing him well enough. With Senator Clinton being the "default candidate" of the Democratic constituency, Senator Obama has an uphill battle during all primaries. Both this point and the caucus argument are moot, however, when the rules of the process are set. And, furthermore, in the specific case of the Clinton/Obama race, Senator Obama is still ahead by any count.

I write this early on Tuesday March 11, 2008 in the morning, before the Mississippi primary.[4] A quick analysis of voting numbers shows Senator Obama leading in number of primary votes 51 percent to 49 percent. When Florida and Michigan are added to the primary vote count, Senator Clinton is leading in votes cast. But let us review this issue more closely.

Senator Clinton won Michigan with 55 percent of the vote. In an uncontested election, you would hope she would do better than slightly more than half. With no other name on the ballot, with her high-profile status, and with the "momentum" of her early New Hampshire victory, that 55 percent is not very good. The current spin on this result is that "you run against uncommitted, that is the toughest election to win" (Rendell 2008).

Regarding Florida, as a resident of the state I was aware that Clinton was campaigning here (Scott, A. 2008). The number of times that she was in the area doing "fundraising events,"—some of which in fact could only be interpreted as political rallies for which people paid a small fee to attend (Schumacher-Matos 2007)—and her many other visits for various reasons were significant. No other Democratic candidate spent more time in Florida before the primary (and none—not even her—after the primary and before the nomination), and she headed a primary victory party in the state (Liasson 2008). Bending the rules seems to be part of her campaign strategy, and we have had enough of rule-bending presidents.

The reality is that Senator Obama leads at this time in valid votes cast in primary elections and in caucus elections, and he leads in pledged delegates and states won (table 1). The argument that the states that Senator Clinton has won are, in essence, "more equal" than Obama's is specious. When Governor Rendell says that Senator Clinton has won in states that constitute a total amount of electoral votes greater than the states won by Senator Obama he makes a point. But, is he really suggesting that these states (for example, New York) will not be in the Democrat column come November unless Clinton is the nominee? He claims that many of the states Senator Obama has won will likely represent Republican Electoral College votes, and in many cases this may be true. It will almost certainly be true with Clinton against McCain, but it is not so clear with Obama against McCain. Obama, for example, won the South Carolina primary—a traditional red state—with a number of votes for all Democrats greater than the aggregate Republican vote for the same state early in their primary process.[5]

Senator Obama has changed the rules of campaigning, attracting new voters, minimizing personal attacks, reaching out to outsiders, reestablishing fundraising patterns, and generally campaigning to position his own credibility as a leader without attempting to diminish the stature of his opponent. Senator McCain seems to have noticed this campaign style, and has sometimes tried to emulate it. These are the new rules of the game. On the other hand, by refusing to recognize this electoral national sentiment, Senator Clinton's tactics at this time could be working to destroy an opportunity to seize a chance at a new era in politics for the Democratic Party. If she becomes the Democratic nominee, her focus on her husband's style of half-plus-one politics will make Senator McCain the next president of the United States, as disenchanted new Democrats will skip the polls or will vote for Ralph Nader.

Open Letter to Senator Obama

March 26, 2008

Shortly after the Super Tuesday debacle for Senator Clinton (February 5), and after a string of wins by Senator Obama in small caucuses and states, the Reverend Wright issue came to the forefront. Despite the

Table 1
Summary of Primary Voting Results as of March 11, 2008
(Not Including Mississippi)

Total Votes for Senators Clinton and Obama
- Total votes cast (includes MI and FL):   27,727,713 total votes
- All primaries to date: 27,032,766 primary votes
- All caucuses to date: 694,947 caucus votes
- All votes including estimated MI votes for Obama*:   27,875,351 total votes
- Michigan votes for Clinton: 378,309 votes
- Florida votes for Clinton and Obama: 1,447,200 votes
- All votes minus Michigan: 27,349,404 votes
- All votes minus Florida: 26,280,513 votes
- All votes minus Michigan and Florida: 25,902,204 valid votes

Hillary Clinton
- Total votes received (includes MI and FL):   13,897,830 votes
                                                (50.12 percent of all votes cast)

- All primaries to date: 13,634,107 primary votes
                                                (50.43 percent)

- All caucuses to date: 263,723 caucus votes
                                                (37.94 percent)

- All votes including MI votes for Obama*:   13,897,830 total votes
                                                (49.85 percent of category)

- All votes minus Michigan: 13,519,521 votes
                                                (49.43 percent of category)

- All votes minus Florida: 13,026,844 votes
                                                (49.57 percent of category)

- All votes minus Florida and Michigan: 12,649,135
                                                (48.83 percent of valid votes)

Barack Obama
- Total votes received: 13,829,883
                                                (49.87 percent in category**)

- All primaries to date: 13,398,659 primary votes
                                                (49.56 percent)

- All caucuses to date: 431,224 caucus votes
                                                (62.05 percent)

- All votes plus Michigan Obama votes*:   13,977,521
                                                (50.14 percent in category)

- All votes minus Michigan: 13,829,883
                                                (50.56 percent in category)

- All votes minus Florida**:   13,253,669
                                                (50.43 percent in category)

- All votes minus Florida and Michigan: 13,253,669
                                                (51.16 percent of valid votes)

Table 1 (cont.)

Clearly, while a virtual tie at this point, Michigan is the trump card for Clinton in all these numbers. In the most favorable calculation for Clinton, the difference in total votes received at the time of preliminary results was 158,996, approximately the minimum estimated vote for Obama in Michigan.*** Since the argument a few weeks ago was that the popular vote could and should be trumped by super delegate decisions, it now seems disingenuous to argue that Clinton has achieved popular vote majority (albeit including Michigan and Florida) and thus entitled to the nomination. It is unlikely that Obama will not overcome that difference in the remaining contests.

Notes

*   Estimated attributed Michigan vote is 25 percent of votes cast in the primary (Total votes in MI 590,553; attributed to Senator Obama: 147,638 votes). Senator Obama has not gathered less than 25 percent of the vote in any primary held to date.

**   Michigan not included as Senator Obama was not on the ballot.

***   This difference at certification for the Denver convention was 67,947 votes.

Source: CNN Election Center (all counts updated to final certified results)

fact that some of these videos had been around for a while by then, their existence was brought into the spotlight at this time, with the Republican nominee already selected and with Senator Clinton behind in the Democratic race. No one knows for sure who was responsible for the high exposure of the "revelations." It could have been conservative pundits or conservative media, which certainly did give great exposure to Rev. Wright's videos and sound bites; it could have come from the Republican side, beginning their Rovian tactics; or it could have come from Clintonites in Chicago. In the end, Rev. Wright used this limelight to burn up his fifteen minutes of fame, revealing himself as an anachronistic throwback to the black activism of the sixties, frozen in time and ideas. He has not understood the changes that have grown around him, using the pulpit for self-aggrandizment and dismissive of the possibility of Senator Obama's election. The Rev. Wright issue was the beginning of more subversive attacks on Senator Obama, as Senator Clinton's campaign went from front-runner status to a fight for survival.[6]

At that time, I wrote an open letter to Senator Obama and emailed it to friends, family, and others, including Senator Obama's own "personal" campaign email address.[7]

Dear Senator Obama:

I do not really expect you to read this letter at this time, and I certainly do not expect to receive any acknowledgment for it. Still, I need to write it. You must have heard it already many times, but it bears repeating that—framed within the objective of refocusing bias, prejudice and racism into a discussion on how to communicate about each other's fears, misconceptions and stereotypes—your Philadelphia Race Relations "A More Perfect Union" speech encourages a national self-introspective process that is part and parcel of what leadership is all about; and I wholeheartedly believe that this process is good for America. [8]

As an American born abroad, and having lived many years in Latin America, I have personally experienced these types of cultural gaps and ideological misconceptions regarding our country; the kind of gaps and misconceptions that have created a World view of America from abroad to which our country sometimes seems witless.

The mainstream view in the U.S. that, although misunderstood by the World we are fundamentally good is, unfortunately, not entirely shared. Rev. Wright's September 16, 2001 incendiary remarks about 9/11 that ended with "...the chickens have come home to roost," are an echo from abroad and, as uncomfortable as they make us feel, they beget a discussion that we need to eventually have in America.

Senator Obama, I believe that your formative years in an environment not entirely unlike the one in which I was raised, allow you to understand these cultural gaps. The gaps generated by America's modern "original sins."[9]

The modern sins that the World at large generally holds us accountable for include the massive killings of civilians in a major dramatic strike on Hiroshima the morning of August 6, 1945 and, more unforgivably, in Nagasaki two days later, birthing the might of modern America for years to come. Outside America's mainstream thought, these events are characterized as genocidal actions. The hundreds of thousands of deaths in the firebombing of Dresden and Tokyo in the middle of a few nights has not fully been addressed yet either, except in a superficial way. The trampling of children and villagers in South East Asia is still glossed over. To say that these actions were necessary to save American lives is not enough. It is also necessary to be candid about the fact that these actions killed innocent non-Americans, and that our sentiments and sympathies do go beyond a "collateral damage" rationalization, while suggesting the existence of second or third-class world citizens that can be bought off with a fist full of dollars.

We may not be ready for this discussion in America, and no leader may be able to politically survive an open discussion on these issues at this time. But, at some future point, the U.S. will have to apologize publicly and sincerely, atoning to the World just as Germany seems to continuously do for WWII and the Holocaust, and as Japan has begun, tentatively and vacillating, for its actions before and during WWII.

To end the increasing isolation and perceived arrogance of America, the dialogue may need to begin with a reckoning of some of our sins to the World. And, as Rev. Wright's "unpatriotic" 9/11 statements shockingly reveal to us—and similar remarks with different phrasing occasionally come out from other public figures dismissively characterized as "extreme left" and "nuts" such as Rosie O'Donnell and Michael Moore—there is a need for an internal healing on this issue. Hopefully Senator Obama, given your Philadelphia speech, today we may be closer to the beginning of that healing process; we may be moving forward towards a more perfect union, not just in better touch with ourselves but also closer to the world around us.

Senator Barack Obama and the World Man

April 11, 2008

R. Buckminster Fuller, the inventor, architect, philosophical thinker, and author wrote forty years ago that it was probable that the "world man" of the future would look like a moderately tall, tan-skinned person, perhaps with an appearance much like that of a native from Central America or the Middle East (Fuller 1969). When all the blood of the world was mixed, he stated, future men will share "every type of human characteristic and every known physiognomy, each of which [will] occur in such a variety of skin shades from black to white that they [will] not permit the ignorance-invented 'race' distinctions predicated only superficially on extreme limits of skin color" (Fuller 1969: Section 8).

Why is this notion relevant to our world today? Forty years after those words we are still many years away from such a world. In fact, our children's children may never be or see that future "world man" of Bucky's. But it is undeniable that our national gene pool is varied now and will remain so. Our culture is commingled now and will only become more so. We are now multicultural and multiracial, and I believe that is the source of our strength and our future advantage. It is in America's mixed roots and rich cultural background where our present lies, and where our future will be built upon.

Senator Barack Obama's heritage parallels America's heritage. Besides having a rich gene pool of his own, Obama was fortunate to be raised in an environment of multicultural diversity. Living in Indonesia during formative years, in Hawaii as a minority student within a stratified social environment, and on the U.S. mainland as a black man, Senator Obama has been forged with the opportunity to participate, observe, and bridge many points of view: from the privileged to the oppressed, and from the powerful to the destitute. He is uniquely positioned at this time in our history as a liaison between cultures, religions, races, and generations.

Our country's roots touch and reach many countries and continents. Our influence on the world and of the world on us is ubiquitous. And in America now, even though we are so diverse, we strive to live within principles of interactive coexistence and tolerance. It seems, and I have the "audacity to hope," that Senator Obama recognizes these facts and wants to use them to lead America into the future. I believe that Senator Obama best represents the "world man" for America today. He seems to understand the need to reassert America's paradigm of mixed ideals, roots and visions to our present social reality. That is why I support Senator

Barack Obama for the next president of the United States of America. His potential capacity to listen, to understand, and to empathize is what leads me to believe that he will be a positive force for America. He has the potential to merge multiple approaches towards a common goal of a decent life for all, leading America to a better place, a respected place among a community of nations and a place of proud self-respect for all Americans.

Notes

1. Interestingly, Senator McCain, who in March had a similar, issue-driven campaign outlook, reverted to the tactics of extreme attacks towards the end of his presidential campaign.

2. These are references to President Bill Clinton's many alleged affairs, including the one with Ms. Lewinsky, the allegations of allowing major campaign donors to stay in the Lincoln Bedroom, "Travelgate" (the firing of the White House travel staff in order to place old-time cronies in charge of the travel arrangements of top government executives), the Whitewater land development, and the Hsi Lai Buddhist Temple in the Los Angeles 1996 campaign contributions scandal.

3. First mentioned in *Meet the Press* with Tim Russert on February 24, 2008. Nader's actual words in context were as follows: MR. RUSSERT: How would you feel, however, if Ralph Nader's presence on the ballot tilted Florida or Ohio to John McCain and McCain became president, and Barack Obama, the first African-American who had been nominated by the Democratic Party—this is hypothetical—did not become president and people turned to you and said, "Nader, you've done it again"? MR. NADER: Not a chance. If the Democrats can't landslide the Republicans this year, they ought to just wrap up, close down, and emerge in a different form. You think the American people are going to vote for a pro-war John McCain who almost gives an indication that he's the candidate of perpetual war, perpetual intervention overseas? You think they're going to vote for a Republican like McCain, who allies himself with the criminal, recidivistic regime of George Bush and Dick Cheney, the most multipliable impeachable presidency in American history? (Nader 2008)

4. The results for the Mississippi primary were: Obama 61.2 percent (265,502 votes), Clinton 36.7 percent (159,221 votes) (Cassreino 2008).

5. In the South Carolina primaries, Senator Obama gathered 295,214 votes, winning by a 28.9 percent margin over Senator Clinton and 55.4 percent of the total votes. There were a total of 532,468 votes in the Democratic Party SC primaries. The Republican Party total number of primary votes for SC was 445,499, and Senator McCain garnered 147,686 of these (33.15 percent). Eventually, in the general election 1,920,969 votes were cast in SC, of which 44.9 percent went to Senator Obama, and 53.9 percent went to Senator McCain.

6. Even though Senator McCain said his campaign would not use the Rev. Wright issue—perhaps because of his own previous troubles with church leaders—at least one political action committee ran attack ads tying Senator Obama to Rev. Wright. The television ads ran during the first week of November over a banner of *"Hate we can believe in"*—a variation on Obama's campaign slogan *"Change we can believe in."*

7. This letter and the following essay *"Senator Barack Obama and the World Man"* made clear to my friends and family who I supported and why. The immediate

reaction was one of passionate conversation, and everyone I sent it to switched sides or reaffirmed their position in favor of Obama.

8.   I encourage anybody who has not done so to read a transcript of Senator Obama's "A More Perfect Union" speech.

9.   The commonly named "original sins" of America are slavery and the genocide of American Indians, particularly as driven by Manifest Destiny. Slavery and its consequent legacy of bigotry, racism and poverty was the main theme around which the classic film *Birth of a Nation* by D. W. Griffith was developed, in what could be described as a white supremacist view. The legacy of the American Indian tragedy includes territorial and economic isolation, poverty, stereotyping and misunderstandings to this day.

2

Clinton vs. Obama

The Pennsylvania primary (April 22) was extremely hard fought and, with Senator Edwards out of contention, it was a major test for Senator Obama. He lost by a difference of about 9.6 percent. The media and the Clinton campaign rounded this figure up to 10 percent, a number that had been touted before as the "magical number" that would purportedly indicate that Senator Obama was greatly weakening (Rutenberg 2008). The Pennsylvania campaign included a barrage of negative ads, as well as many changes in position from the Clinton side, depending on where the rallies were held; old-style politics at its worst.

After Pennsylvania: What are the Rules of the Game?

April 23, 2008

The heat of the moment may make us sometimes forget a bit about history. The buzz-and-rumor seeding by campaign spinmasters are designed to make us ask the question "why can't he put her away?" suggesting that he has weakened. However, maybe the question begs to be asked from the other side: "why can't *she* put him away?"

An upstart junior senator from a Midwestern state whose principal claim to fame when he started the process was, yes, a speech in a friendly, pepped-up Democratic convention; an African American with very little funding and even less political capital behind him. How could she lose against him? Furthermore, how could she lose against him by that much? What does that say about her own strength and political base?

The answer may lie in the different rules of the numbers games: old politics rules vs. new politics rules. The numbers she garnered at the start do show that she is the strongest candidate in the old politics game: the game of overt and surreptitious negative campaigning, the game of political machine grinding, the game of shameless pandering and localized flip-flopping. The demographics do show that this game has worked for her: yes, she is stronger according to old politics. But, is this still the real political moment we are living in? Or is this perhaps the last dying gasp of an out-of-touch, distant way of doing politics, a message-managing style that was effective before the existence of twenty-four-hour cable news cycles, YouTube, Google, texting, and the blogosphere? At this point in the game, the only thing certain is that the new politics is getting a hard lesson in old politics. Hopefully, it will not make us all overly cynical and turn us off.

How Electable Will the Democratic Candidate Be?

April 30, 2008

The potential weaknesses of both senators Clinton and Obama as candidates in the general election need to be explored. There are issues in both candidates' backgrounds that can be negatively framed—as a matter of fact, there are probably issues in anybody's background that can be negatively spun if need be. By no means do I believe that either candidate is what these potential lines of attack suggest. Both candidates are vulnerable, however, to scathing and derisive attacks from the Republican side.

The issue of electability, which is being argued right now by the ultimate deciding constituency—the superdelegates—goes directly to the question that Senator Clinton is trying to raise as substantive: *"Do we know everything that we need to know about Senator Obama?"*

That is, by every right, a legitimate question. To a great extent, however, this question has been answered already. The scrutiny, the spotlight, the research, the inquiries, and the doubts about Senator Obama have been raised and addressed already in many ways, and more than once. On the other hand, many real issues affecting Senator Clinton's electability have not been raised yet at all. The Republican Attack Machine (as she describes it) is simply lying in wait, with her dossier already prepared, and gladly receiving contributions to Senator Obama's dossier.

To understand the issue of electability, let us review the candidates' publicly available information, information that, in both cases, can de distorted to create reasonable doubts.

Obama Under Attack:
1.   *He is inexperienced.* He's been an elected official for seven years in the "most average State in the U.S." (Ohlemacher 2007). He's been a U.S. senator since 2004. His opponents dropped out of the races—after he challenged their legal standing as candidates—so it has been argued that he has not really run for office in a hostile environment and cannot

coordinate such an ambitious endeavor.[1] His only previous executive experience is, first as a junior researcher in a firm helping Americans do business abroad, then taking the risky role of an amorphous "community organizer" during the early 1980s and again in the 1990s. His experience as a lawyer is confined to work related to discrimination, voter registration, assisting on the legal issues of publicly funded community projects and as a constitutional law professor (Obama 1995, 2004, 2006).

2. *We do not really know who he is.* We only found out about him in 2004, when he introduced John Kerry during the Democratic Party Convention, making a "pretty speech." It is argued that his charisma only comes from his persuasive rhetoric, his skill in talking and, perhaps, a "black guilt" within "liberal America."

3. *He is different from us.* His background includes possible Muslim ties and possible radical black racist sympathies. He has associates and sympathies with people with radical views; he knows extremists, and maybe will befriend more of them in the future. He has links to felonious Chicago characters. These, and who knows who else, may have funded his campaign for the Illinois State Senate, as well as those of other prominent "Chicago Politicians." Of the close to $100 million raised to date for Obama's campaign, approximately $2.5 million have been linked to political action committees and lobbyists.

4. *He is weak.* Some argue that he seems incapable of fighting back and standing on his own when attacked, fairly or unfairly. They state that his lack of spine is a fatal character flaw. His style of dialogue, which could be seen as constructive, conciliatory and as reaching out to the "enemy," is also seen as vulnerable and naïve. His position that direct and forceful action as a first option may be reckless, is viewed by some as an indication of someone who is afraid of confrontation.

Actually, the limited extent to which Senator Obama can be attacked is claimed to be a measure of his short career and his possible hidden flaws. It is clear that most of these attack points are red herrings seeking to misinform (i.e., "he is Muslim" and similar) and confound. They are based on creating a fear of the (supposedly) unknown.

On the other hand, and given the longer public history of Senator Clinton and her husband, there is a large amount of information circulating that can be used to attack her. Information in many cases distorted out of the original facts, or simple reflections on her character and history spun with a negative twist. Such spin can be presented very negatively and unfairly, as follows.

Clinton Under Attack

1. *Her experience is not real.* She has only seven years of experience in elected office. Her White House experience, as revealed by her disclosed

schedule (Nicholas & Leavey 2008), does not make her "ready from day one" in the way it is claimed—unless hers is actually a reelection of Bill Clinton in disguise. As a first lady, she did not participate in Cabinet meetings and did not have top security clearance. Her critics (in an openly sexist slight) highlight how her duties included creating a new sculpture garden and redecorating the Treaty Room and the Blue Room. During her White House years she did have a constant role as liaison between each end of Pennsylvania Avenue and that, again, can be spun negatively or positively. She broke the record that Pat Nixon had of most traveled first lady, jet setting in political junkets to over seventy countries. Again, positive or negative? In Arkansas, she practiced law, specializing on defending big corporations from patent and copyright infringement. As a Wal-Mart board member, it is claimed she did nothing on record regarding the labor practices of this Arkansas based corporation (Barbaro 2007), despite in fact breaking (or at least cracking) the glass ceiling for executive women in that corporation.

2. *She is driven by "extreme liberal" values.* Her advocacies for children's rights include establishing the right of children to sue their parents (Depalma 1992), which may be, once again, a contentious issue easily spun into a way that makes her go into defensive mode. Given her strong pro-choice stance, a position she has already been targeted on, she will be depicted as a "New York Left-Wing Liberal."

3. *She is driven by "extreme ambition."* Some have claimed that her move to Arkansas to live with Bill Clinton was motivated by political ambition and by her frustrations after failing in DC on her own (Gerth, Van Natta, Jr. 2007). It is also said that their marriage a year later was intended to enhance his political career (Gerth, ibid, , Bernstein 2007).[2] They had previously lived together as students at Yale and in California, when she interned for a San Francisco law firm which included Black Panther extremists as clients and members of the Communist Party as partners, creating further opportunities to smear her by association.[3] She kept her Rodham surname when marrying Clinton in order to define her individual career, but it will be claimed that she has now leveraged her husband's name for political gain, and that his is an influence that she covets over any moral qualms regarding his alleged relationships with numerous other women.[4] Her move to New York will once again be said to have been ambitious carpetbag posturing to leverage herself as a viable presidential candidate, instead of out of any particular loyalty to her future New York constituency.[5]

4. *Her deals have not always been transparent.* There are some financial and management issues in her background that may be spun as less than virtuous: brought to light again will be the spectacular and never fully explained $100,000 return on a $10,000 investment in cattle futures within ten months (Gerth & Van Natta, Jr. 2007), and the convoluted dealings of Whitewater with its associated failure of Madison Guaranty Savings & Loan at taxpayers' expense. Her hand was also claimed to

be involved in the firing of the White House Travel Office (that coordinated her trips to those "over seventy countries"), allegedly to hire friends of the Clintons (Safire 1996, 2000 among others).

5. *Her campaign financing has not always been transparent.* Questions in this area can be very damaging for Senator Clinton. For example: the use of her foreign connections may have included raising campaign donations from China (this refers to the potentially damaging allegations regarding the Hsi Lai Buddhist Temple in Los Angeles in 1996 and her alleged role in this scandal). It may be alleged that some of these or other donors and friends of donors got a chance to sleep in the Lincoln Bedroom in exchanges for favors or special treatment. It will be asked, to what extent will "pardonees" of President Clinton and Clinton Library or Foundation donors have any kind of influence in a new Clinton co-presidency.

6. *She is not truthful.* Senator Clinton has been called out on truth distortions, half-truths, and outright lies. This could be damaging for her campaign. William Safire called her "a congenital liar" and a "habitual prevaricator" comparing her to the dark sides of Richard Nixon (Safire 1996, 2000). Robert Ray, special counsel in charge of investigating the White House Travel Office scandal, concluded that she had "given false testimony" in the case, trying to minimize her role in this affair. And her campaign claims about snipers in Bosnia were quickly discredited by news footage clips of the trip in question.

7. *She is vindictive.* This is sexist code for the "B word" among her detractors. It is claimed that she used the FBI to investigate her enemies (Safire 2000), comparing her to Richard Nixon and Herbert Hoover in the uses and abuses of power. It is claimed that she leveraged her connections and power on party officials directly and indirectly to obtain superdelegates and machinery support, exercising political heavy-handed clout and favors to an unprecedented extent, yet sowing resentment within some party members. The rumors that she suggested to her supporters that they should vote for McCain if she were to lose to Senator Obama so that she could have a chance in 2012 are slanderous and most likely untrue, but almost sound credible given the distorted allegations about her character.

In evaluating these weaknesses and potential attacks to each candidate, Senator Clinton's balance is not favorable. The Republicans have a deep well to draw from to attack her, again possibly because of a longer public trajectory than Senator Obama's. Her own style and these weaknesses could also make the fall campaign extremely negative if she is the presidential candidate. This election is for the Democrats to lose, and electability only becomes an issue if the Democratic Party leadership makes it so.

Notes

1. In comparing the management of Senator Obama' campaign with Senator Clinton's it seems that on her side there was much more disarray: on February 10 2008, Hillary Clinton's campaign manager Patti Solis Doyle was ousted. On April 6, Clinton's campaign chief strategist Mark Penn resigned, ostensibly over conflicts of interest regarding Colombia, but suspiciously after the gains made by Senator Obama during the primaries. The strategy used by Senator Clinton of focusing on Super Tuesday, disregarding caucus states, is (perhaps wrongly) attributed to Penn.

2. A year before, in 1974, Bill Clinton lost his first attempt at running for political office, U.S. Congress, Arkansas 3rd Congressional District.

3. In the summer of 1971 Hillary Clinton interned at the Oakland, California, law firm of Treuhaft, Walker, and Burnstein. Robert E. Treuhaft was a Communist Party member from the 1940s to 1958.

4. In an interesting article regarding books by or about the candidates, *Time* magazine compares unauthorized biographies of Mrs. Clinton by Jeff Gerth and Don Van Natta, Jr. (*Her Way: The Hopes and Ambitions of Hillary Rodham Clinton* [Little, Brown and Company, 2007]) and Carl Bernstein (*A Woman in Charge* [Alfred A. Knopf, 2007]). In both it is alleged that the marriage was originally one of political convenience. The comparison is available on-line at *Time/CNN: The Candidates in Prin.*

5. http://www.time.com/time/2007/candidates_books/clinton/.

6. In fact, and perhaps to counter this charge but probably more out of her authentic political roots and background as first lady in Arkansas and of the U.S., Senator Clinton worked hard to be a senator for *all* New York State, more so than previous ones who mostly leveraged their New York City base (Horowitz 2008).

3

A Pair of Primary Issues

As the primaries unfolded, and Senator Obama took the lead, his focus began to shift towards Senator McCain's campaign. There are many issues that defined differences between Obama and McCain, and I sent portions or extracts of these complex essays to publications, such as the *Los Angeles Times* and the *Miami Herald*, as well as to personalities such as Robert Reich and David Axelrod.

Let's Talk About Unemployment

April 30, 2008

The Bush administration had the claim of achieving one if not the longest low open unemployment rate streaks in recent American history. The unemployment rate is defined by the number of people that, as a percentage of the work force, are actively looking for a job while currently without one. Until as recently as the 1990s, many economists' traditional view was that anything between 5 to 6 percent meant an economy in "full employment," meaning by that a representation of the natural turnaround of people quitting or getting fired and reentering the job market and new job seekers. Now, low unemployment is not necessarily always a positive indicator. There could actually be "too much employment" in an economy. Lower than 5 percent unemployment rates could mean an overheated job market, sparking salary inflation and consequently general inflation. The U.S. unemployment rates of less than 4 percent, 3 percent over the last few years, with low inflation or less, however, defied this conventional view.[1]

As with many assumptions regarding the market and the economy, these numbers now need to be viewed under "New Economy" rules: an economy that encourages low-cost outsourcing, technological quasi-efficiencies, and quick obsolescence. In fact, what has occurred is that this new economy of recent years has led to an economy of discouragement and discontent; an economy that forces people to leave the job market or discourages attempts to join it; an economy that has increased real inefficiencies and decreased the whole value of the job market when compared to GDP growth[2]; an economy that has decreased standards of living, from basic services and staples, to issues such as health care and security; an economy that has made us all worse off; an economy that has eroded the value of education and pushed off the notion of retirement for many.

Just because people are forced to eke out a living with whatever means they can scramble together at any given point, it does not mean that they feel "employed." Families opening and closing mom-and-pops, selling classified coupons in their neighborhood newspaper, advertising used items out of their garage through Ebay, in so many cases expending more than what they make, are not a demonstration of resourcefulness but a demonstration of a failed economy. These people may not be counted among the statistically unemployed but, after all, they are.

In an economy based on low-costing there is hardly any job value created and the productivity gains are more indicative of this than of better standards of living. Market inefficiencies run galore, losing educational and training investment, and the real winners are the credit card companies that finance many failed family enterprises—as well as the bankruptcy lawyers—while credit card protection reform languishes in Congress, awaiting the next great financial crisis. Family breadwinners in this situation are not unemployed but are underemployed, underutilized by a society that has destroyed opportunity by relentlessly giving breaks and incentives to big corporations, and by making it harder and harder for mid-size and small businesses to survive.

Our economy is faltering in many fronts.[3] A new vision is required to begin to sort out the problems and move towards solutions, jumping the gun, outside the box or with whatever cliché suits the speech of the moment. As Americans, we can only hope that our next president is a person capable of identifying that new vision.

Many in America are in a bad employment situation, having invested money in an education that is now worthless, surviving on the fringes of the old economy, and with bleak future prospects. For many, these issues are not academic platitudes or political discussions, but life itself. The vision of a better future is cloudy for most of us, but it is obvious that recognizing the uncertainty of the future is much better than receiving comfort from a misinterpreted past and believing it should simply be replicated with some minor tweaking.

I do not wish to be presumptuous regarding these notions, as many are much better informed about these matters than I am. But I need to express the anxieties that are glossed over when the Republican candidate claims that everything is actually better than it was before.[4]

Our Health Care Market Dilemma

May 3, 2008

Economists have a clear way of labeling the underlying structural problem of today's American health care system: market failures. Within free markets, the microeconomic theory of supply and demand works well for commodity products and services. In perfect markets, with perfect information and universal access, products and services are priced at their true economic value and providers of a product or service are rewarded according to this true value, making zero extraordinary profits over market value. The key words here are "perfect markets." Businesses are rewarded above the market value of their products and services when they can find market imperfections and take advantage of them, by creating various types of monopolies. That is the way our economy works.

Information and location monopolies are typical ways in which market imperfections are exploited. To encourage investment, these imperfections are sometimes protected by the regulating authority, so information may get protected by copyrights or patents in order to stimulate innovation, and location may be protected by zoning or licensing in order to ensure that services are provided or products are offered, stimulating entrepreneurial risk.

Supply monopolies are a different matter. If a supplier or various suppliers can control supply together, extraordinary profits over market value can be extracted to the detriment of the consumer. In order to avoid unfair monopoly advantages and to encourage competition, antitrust laws are in place.

Most products and services fall within a competitive market structure, providing economic value equilibrium to the consumer through direct supply/demand corrections created by market forces and by adequate oversight. But certain services such as phone, electricity, and general infrastructure fall under the "natural monopoly" category that requires extra oversight and regulation. They are "natural monopolies" because, in order to be economically efficient, they cannot and should not be ruled by normal microeconomic supply-and-demand laws. The difficulty in regulating these natural monopolies has to do with the pricing of "extraordinary profits" over market value. Other services and products are even harder to price or provide under absolute free market rules. These kinds of services fall totally outside market categories of supply and demand, generating "natural" market failures.

For example, if security were allowed to be dictated by supply and demand, the wealthiest minority segment of the population would have private police and armies, while the greater majority would live in an unsafe environment. That is why we have local police, highway patrol, FBI, CIA, the military, and so on. It is in the general interest for all of society that security and law enforcement services be provided by the government. Obviously, these are not free of charge, as anyone who pays real estate taxes and income taxes knows, but they are priced at a substantially lesser global cost for everybody than it would be if its costs had to be individually borne. Society is better off when government takes over and regulates our personal security than it would be if each individual had to take personal responsibility for all their security and law enforcement needs. This is an example of a market failure, where the market cannot provide, in an economically efficient way, a clear societal need. In an unregulated market of security services, providers would try to minimize their exposure by protecting the safest places at the highest possible price. It is cheaper for all members of society in direct as well as indirect costs if government is in charge of security. The economy and society in general is better off with this arrangement.[5]

A healthy population is also a boon for society. The market is more productive under these conditions, and more value is created for all, in a more cost effective way. It is good for society that smallpox has been eradicated for all, and not only for the ones who could afford it. It is good for society that flu season has a minimal effect on productivity (CNN Money 2003, Reuters 2008a).[6] It would be good for society if people could adapt to and cope better with their daily anxieties. Why is it that health care cannot be recognized as a basic social service, then? As a population's health increases so would productivity and general market and societal value. Value creation in a healthy society is greater than in an unhealthy one, and that should be clear for all to see, so it is in a society's best interest to maintain its members in as healthy a state as possible.

The value of a healthy society is a general benefit, a benefit for all members of the society, but health care is typical of situations that create market failures because, when left to the unregulated free market, the value of health care will be appropriated by the suppliers. As in the case of security, when left unregulated to the market forces of supply and demand, only the ones who need it least and are able to pay the most will be the ones able to obtain the service. The tendency in such a situation is that prices will increase over the value of the services, and providers will prefer to offer services to those who need it least—those who offer the lowest risk and the highest profit. In other words, the providers will appropriate the value that is created by a healthy society.

The Commonwealth Fund—a private foundation dedicated to researching health care access and quality—has recent reports on trends of health care in the U.S. The number of 46 to 47 million people uninsured is one that has been bandied around, but the fact is that in 2007 an estimated 116 million adults (ages nineteen to sixty-four) were uninsured, underinsured, reported a medical bill problem, and/or did not access needed health care because of its cost (Collins, et al. 2008). This number represents over 65 percent of all adults in the U.S. in the prime of their working years. Two-thirds of the population has health insurance-related problems be it no coverage, claim disputes, or simple apprehension of the system raising its price if they file a claim; and this trend has increased dramatically over the last few years (see figure 1).

Figure 1
An Estimated 116 Million Adults Were Uninsured, Underinsured,
Reported a Medical Bill Problem, and/or Did Not Access Needed
Health Care Because of Cost, 2007

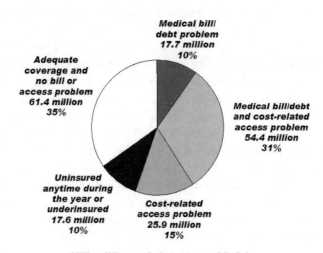

177 million adults, ages 19–64

Source: The Commonwealth Fund Biennial Health Insurance Survey (2007).

Source: Collins et al. 2008

Let us talk in layman terms. In the U.S., the insurance companies are the gatekeepers to health care. When insurance companies have all the power to decide who can benefit from the health care system, the possible benefits that a healthy society could generate for itself are transformed into profits above fair market value for the gatekeeper. This is the classical case of a supply monopoly, because the gatekeeper (the insurance company) gets to decide to whom and at what price the service shall be supplied. However, instead of increasing the health of the overall society, this system generates what economists call "perverse incentives," because it discourages many from paying for their own health care, hence decreasing overall societal health, and free riding on the public health system, increasing inefficiencies all around. The system becomes an elitist system with only a few willing to participate directly investing and benefiting from "the best health care in the world" as our medical services are often called.

As an illustrative, simplified example, let us suppose an entire population universe of one hundred people requires insurance, and they pay $1 for it. Out of this universe, in year 1, five people will require health care services, costing $10 each. This represents a total cost to the insurance company of $50, resulting in a $50 gross profit. Within a free market environment it is the insurance company's responsibility and mission to maximize profits, so the company will now do three things simultaneously: (1) try to lower the cost of health services provided; (2) try to increase the charge for the insurance service; and (3) try to eliminate the five people who are creating costs. It would be better for the insurer, economically speaking, if insurance services in year 2 were only provided to fifty people for $2 each and only one required health care services for $5, resulting in a $95 gross profit. The likelihood is that net profits would also increase, because of the smaller overhead required in the management of fifty insured individuals, as opposed to one hundred individuals. In both years the market paid $100, but the health value has been appropriated by the insurance company and the society in general is worse off. A total of $45 of health value has been transferred by society to the insurance company, possibly through inferior care, lost wages and productivity, and through shifting costs to municipalities (free riding). This is a typical market failure situation, and only by extreme regulation or a complete restructuring of the way health care service is provided can the situation be remedied.

Extreme regulation is inefficient though, and trying to regulate the health care industry as currently structured will only lead to greater societal costs, more free riding and greater value transfers to the health care gatekeepers. The economic incentives within this market take us to the logical conclusion that fewer people at a higher price will receive lower-quality care in the future. The industry's structure, as it stands, leads to insurance companies going out of business if they do not recognize that they have to cater to the healthier and wealthier. This is the way our health care industry works. It is not that evil or shadowy individuals do not care about sick people. It is the structure of the market that leads to this inevitable outcome, and this needs to change.

A major overhaul is required to increase the health value of our society at large. The economic incentives need to be changed for our society to be healthier at a reasonable cost, not less healthy at a higher price. If a major overhaul is not done, cost inefficiencies and free riding will drive programs such as Medicaid, Medicare and state sponsored insurers of last resort into bloated financial sinkholes, while health care in general deteriorates.

Under Senator McCain's health care plan, an inadequate band-aid tries to remedy a structural market failure. Senator Obama's plan proposes a re-structuring that addresses market failures. Perfect solutions are a utopian ideal, but at least we should strive to rectify when an industry's structure is not working and is creating cost inefficiencies and increased hardship on individuals and families. We all agree that 116 million Americans in their most productive years should have adequate healthcare access, as well as younger and older Americans should. The approach to this seemingly intractable issue differentiates the contending parties in this election. In my view, Senator Obama's position seems to recognize the need for a deep structural reform.

Notes

1.   Many economics texts and journal articles elaborate on the concept of natural rate of unemployment and its relationship with inflation. See Milton Friedman, or Joseph Stiglitz, for example.

2.   In the U.S., the increase in average weekly real wages for the private sector from January 2000 to October 2008 was 1.37 percent (Bureau of Labor Statistics 2008). Real GDP growth over the same period was 20.8 percent (Data 360, data360. org).

3.   On December 2, 2008 the National Bureau of Economic Research announced that it had determined that the U.S. had entered a recession beginning December of 2007.

4.   According to *FactCheck.org*, in January 2008 Senator McCain said: "I don't believe we're headed into a recession," and "we've had a pretty good prosperous time, with low unemployment," while also acknowledging that the American economy was in "a rough patch," and that "things are tough right now." In April he said that

"there's been great progress economically" but that the "progress" made during Bush's tenure still wouldn't console American families who are facing "tremendous economic challenges," apparently suggesting that minor changes were required to overcome these challenges. These appear to be contradictory statements and none of them did clearly acknowledge or address the underlying structural economic troubles that surfaced with a vengeance in September 2008.

5.   Other typical cases of market failure include education, where society at large is better off with a better-educated population labor pool, which is the primary economic reason for public education, and interstate roads or bridges, where it is economically more efficient for the government to allow and manage only one toll infrastructure project, rather than have, for example, two toll roads competing for drivers from and to the same destinations.

6.   As reported by Reuters (2008a), the annual cost of the flu season due to productivity lost and medical expenses is estimated at $7 billion, and at 111 million lost workdays. In 2003, CNN Money reported that direct and indirect costs of the flu were estimated between $4 to $15 billion, including 70 million lost workdays (CNN Money 2003).

4

The Primaries are Over—
Election Time is Here

By early May it was clear that the probability of Senator Obama attaining the nomination for his party was very high. I started writing essays and letters considering this as a *fait accompli* and revolving on the role of the Clintons, which I sent to her senatorial office, among others. Strategic electoral decisions were also in play at this time, and the full campaign strategy generated some of these essays, which by the most part were sent only to David Axelrod.

What Now, Clinton?

May 9, 2008

Senator Clinton is a powerful political figure. She obtained nearly a majority of the popular votes in the democratic primaries.[1] She has powerful machinery that allowed her to garner many "super-delegates" from the get-go. She has a strong political brand name that naturally feeds into constituencies of key electoral states. She is not the candidate, however, not anymore. But she is at this time a key member of the Democratic Party team who is required to participate, and participate strongly, if her party wants to win the elections in November. And they do want to win. To think otherwise is to revert to the old divisive politics of needing only half plus one of the total votes in order to win.

The length of the primary season for the Democratic Party has strengthened the candidates' skills and resolve. Senator Obama now goes into the presidential contest as a much better candidate for it. But to guarantee garnering all the Electoral College votes needed, the Democratic Party coalition requires full-hearted support from Senator Clinton. Reviewing the national polls, it seems clear that there are several battleground states in the Obama/McCain contest that would not be as contested in a Clinton/McCain one: Florida, the Rust Belt, and Appalachia.[2] These are around eighty-four Electoral College votes in contention that need to be fought for with the best possible efforts. It is in those states where she could contribute with her capabilities and rally her connections, backers, and supporters to ensure a victory in the fall. Her support and campaigning in these states will help to guarantee a Democratic Party win in the general election.

The difficulty in this scenario is the part that says "what's in it for me?" for Senator Clinton. It seems unlikely that an Obama/Clinton ticket is viable for many reasons, not the least of which is the public animus created between them during the campaign. But personal considerations aside, there are arguments that make this a political liability as well. Senator Obama has convincingly argued that a new set of rules regarding politics should apply, that "old politics" has bogged down government as much as, or more so, than bureaucracy, that a new thinking needs to come to Washington. Having Senator Clinton on the ticket contradicts this argument and undermines one of Senator Obama's greatest assets: his consistency. So, from a political position framework, this "dream ticket" is no such thing. From a political campaign framework, the dream reverts to the Republican National Committee. The amount of disparaging footage that exists and that can be made into a series of ad campaigns showcasing the rivalry between Senator Clinton and Senator Obama could inflict irreparable damage at crucial moments leading to the presidential campaign end-run.

So, it seems that Senator Clinton on this ticket is not the best option. Her best enticement to spend time and effort campaigning for Senator Obama in those crucial states may be the rebuilding of her credibility and position among old Clinton constituencies and among the new constituencies of Senator Obama. This should also happen in order to create ground for who seems to be the next Clinton politician in the pipeline: Chelsea. If she wants it, and by no means is this really clear at this point, Chelsea could be a junior White House staffer, or have some other similar role within an Obama presidency, enabling her to start creating image and credentials for a future political career. The young Clinton could serve as a bridge between the New Democrats and the old politics to help mend the rift between Senator Obama and his supporters and Senator Clinton and her supporters. Senator Clinton may see this potential for her daughter as an additional positive reason to ensure a massive victory by Senator Obama this November.

How Electable is the Democratic Candidate? –Redux

May 13, 2008

Back in April, I wrote an essay titled *"How electable will the Democratic candidate be?"* which discussed the potential lines of attack that Republicans could use against either Democratic candidate at the time, be it Obama or Clinton. With Obama now clearly emerging as the presidential candidate, this new essay explores the same ideas but from the perspective of a national election.

***

David Axelrod, chief campaign strategist for Senator Obama, said today on *Morning Joe* that the senator will try to conduct a campaign from "a different place" meaning by that a campaign focused and driven by issues, and not by attacking character and personalities. However, their strategy cannot be just about being in a different place. Their strategy really does need to address the key attack points against Senator Obama in a viable, "sound-bite" way. These key attack points remain the same, and an answer needs to be on the tip of every tongue in Obama's campaign, replying quickly and effectively to the attacks on Senator Obama, which include answers to such charges as:

1. *He is inexperienced*
    Counterpoints: Twenty-five years dedicated to giving a voice to Americans in need and distress; ten years in elected office including seven years in the fifth most populous state in the nation; three years as U.S. senator of the same state; fifteen years of non-elected experience that shaped his commitment to "the people on the streets" significantly including his role as a community organizer in low-income areas of Chicago. Helped poor Americans during the booming early 1980s "me decade" and returned to the same activities in the early 1990s after graduating with honors from Harvard, with even more skill. His experience as a lawyer during this time is related to ending discrimination, empowering voters, and assisting on the legal issues of publicly funded community projects. He is also an expert on constitutional law, a topic that he taught for many years at a major national university. His current success as a candidate demonstrates that he can effectively and efficiently lead and manage a large-scale bureaucratic enterprise. He effectively reengineered electoral campaigns in the U.S., overtaking the establishment candidate and initially presumptive nominee of his own party, and showcasing how he can bring "change" to an existing archaic and rigid system.
2. *We do not really know who he is or what he may be hiding*
    Counterpoints: As a candidate to the highest office in a protracted campaign, Senator Obama has been more than scrutinized. An adversarial

media has done its best to find out all possible dirt about him. His opponent in the nomination process, Senator Clinton, tried unsuccessfully to uncover issues regarding character, associates, corporate support, etc. Some supposedly "negative associations" he may have are easy to explain, as a result of past activities in which he has successfully reached across ideological, social, and political lines. In reaching across these lines, he has to communicate, he has to relate and he has to know characters and people that may be unsavory generally speaking. His capacity to communicate with these characters is however a plus, not a negative. The consistency of his message over the campaign has shown everybody that his character and values are in tune with mainstream and progressive America. His campaign's funding, direct and indirect, does not come from major quasi-mysterious donors but from millions of people across America.

3.   *He is different from "us"*

It is likely that this line of attack will be the core of attacks to come. This argument has ranged from "he is not black enough" to "he is black" to "he is a Muslim" to "he doesn't care about Israel," and even to "he is un-American." His background, it will be argued, includes possible Muslim ties and possible radical black racist sympathies. He, it will be argued, has associates and sympathies with people with radical views; he knows extremists, and maybe will befriend more of them in the future.

Counterpoints: Clear biographical sound-bites stronger than *"when I worked the South side of Chicago"* are required. High-profile endorsements—and using these in public relations campaigns—and active surrogates within weak constituencies are needed; and perhaps those eventual town hall meetings with Senator McCain could be extremely useful.

4.   *He is incapable of fighting back and standing on his own when attacked, fairly or unfairly. His lack of spine is a fatal character flaw*

Counterpoints: Turning the argument on its head, the rhetoric runs something like this: "Do you really think that because he believes that in order to lead he needs to bring 'the enemy' around to his side, this is a sign of weakness? Do you really think that because he thinks that dialogue is constructive between adversaries, he is naïve? Do you really think that because he thinks that direct and forceful action as a first option may be reckless, he is afraid of confrontation?" The contrast between the current consequences of confrontational leadership and, yes, the "hope" of better results through collaborational leadership can be played up.

A leader, by implicit definition, is different from his followers, but resonates positively within "the gut" of his constituencies. Senator Obama will always be different from the majority of his constituencies, but this is something to embrace, not to reject. What the senator needs to demonstrate is how his goals, values and ideals are, in fact, the same as "ours."

The basis for all these attack points is the fear of the unknown factor. This factor has failed however when by his campaigning voters get to know more about Senator Obama; and has failed in the more intimate caucus processes of the primaries (he's obtained over 64 percent of the caucus delegates in the primaries). Senator Obama is the most diverse candidate, genetically and in upbringing, that America has ever seen. His white ancestry of Midwestern stock, his black ancestry, directly from Africa, and his upbringing in diverse cultures makes him the ideal empathy bridge for diverse and divergent America.

Winning the Election Decisively

May 19, 2008

Senator McCain is a powerful candidate; the Republicans have not lost yet. Senator McCain's strengths are based on his long trajectory of public service, starting in the early 1960s with the U.S. Navy—including combat and administrative positions—and all the way to his four terms as U.S. senator from Arizona. He is the paradigm of a life dedicated to public service with the deserved glory of a war hero, but does that entitle him to be president?

Qualifications are not in question here, the way these will be raised for Senator Obama. The most salient individual traits that could be Senator McCain's potential weaknesses are his reputed temper and his age, both of which can be spun favorably for him in terms of character and experience. A general analysis of electoral votes at this date actually adds up close to, or to a little more, than 270 for Senator McCain.[3] He may not have a majority of the popular vote—as it also seems from the polls—but, when has that stopped anyone from becoming president of the U.S.?

Of course, polls at this time are (almost) meaningless. There is an eternity of change waiting to happen from May to November, and polls will reflect constant change in the intention to vote. A clear path to victory does not rely on intended votes alone.

Senator McCain's path to the nomination made it clear that his greatest strength is also his greatest weakness. The appeal that Senator McCain has for "independents and centrists" (I&Cs) tends to alienate the conservative core of the Republican Party, especially in the Southern states and other conservative constituencies. While Senator Obama will have to fight for the "I&Cs" throughout the country—with potentially greater appeal, given the current state of the nation—it is obvious that the Republican core will not be in play, and will remain Republican. However, that Republican core could be so turned off by its choices that they may simply not show up at the polls. Senator McCain's disparaging remarks about Pat Robertson and Jerry Farwell,[4] for example, may not be remembered at this time but would need to be defended when raised (Knowlton 2000). Many other instances in which the senator was branded a "traitor to the Republican Party" by his colleagues, to the extent that his name was floated as a potential independent candidate or even as a VP for John Kerry, may be remembered. Rush Limbaugh many times denounced McCain, suggesting repeatedly that he was not a "true Republican".[5]

Undoubtedly, it is a prerogative of being human that one can change one's mind, but in the case of Senator McCain's positions he comes pretty close to being a "flip-flopper," seeming to play to the base of the Republican Party for electioneering purposes. These are the kinds of points that, when raised in the southern coalition states, may break the Republican victory.

The core of the southern strategy for Senator Obama may to be to reinforce the questioning Senator McCain's "true Republican" credentials, balanced with a strong push for the independents. McCain's countermeasure will be in his choice for vice president and, because the Republican Convention is scheduled after the Democratic one, he has an advantage there.[6] Thus, timing of the southern state strategy for the Democrats has to be in synch with this fact: it should not begin until after the Republican National Convention.

Notes

1.   Final results as DNC certified by August 20 (reported on the CNN Election Center tracker) gave Senator Clinton 17,675,809 votes, not including Puerto Rico, but including Florida and Michigan. The same results for Senator Obama were 17,556,051 votes. A difference of 119,758 or .34 percent in favor of Clinton. It must be pointed out that Obama did not campaign in Florida or was on the ballot in Michigan. In Puerto Rico, where for the first time ever a presidential candidate campaigned —Senator Clinton—the results were 263,120 Clinton / 121,458 Obama. According to the DNC rules, Puerto Rico votes do not count for the nomination process because, likewise, Puerto Rico votes do not count for the general election, as it has no Electoral College presence. In total valid primaries, Senator Obama received 16,979,837 votes vs. 16,213.394 votes for Senator Clinton (50.98 percent vs. 49.92 percent). In caucuses the results were 486,125 vs. 263,873 delegates (64.83 percent vs. 35.17 percent).

2.   The daily polls of polls tracking national and individual states referred to were tracked on realclearpolitics.com.

3.   For the electoral vote count during the whole election season, and based on polls of polls results, see Appendix 3, which includes graphs developed by electoral-vote.com.

4.   Senator McCain called Falwell and Robertson "agents of intolerance," "corrupting influences on religion and politics," and said parts of the religious right were

divisive and even un-American (Knowlton 2000) while campaigning in 2000, and influenced by their opposition to gambling, as McCain pushed for new tribes and federal gambling rules. Information on McCain and the gambling lobby surfaced during the Abramoff scandal, but a summary can be reviewed in a research article by Becker and Van Natta for the New York Times (Becker, Van Natta 2008).

5. In a widely circulated quote Rush Limbaugh said, before Super Tuesday, that Senator McCain "is in a lot of these places not actually the Republican candidate; he is the candidate of enough Republicans, but independents and moderates and probably even some liberals."

6. On the Republican side, this was obviously an important discussion line. The eventual choice of Governor Palin for vice presidential candidate—four months after this essay was first written and circulated—sought to address this issue but, while solidifying and energizing the base, the Palin choice threw off the independents and centrists, creating the seeds for what would become the "Obama Republicans."

5

One Nation Indivisible

Roots of an Unapologetic Liberal

May 15, 2008

My father was an influential figure who wrote one of the most contro-versial—some say notorious, some say famous—books on the political psyche of Latin American politics and ideology, titled in English *The Latin Americans: Their Love-Hate Relationship with the United States* (Rangel 1977). I always wondered a little about that title, but he told me that the publishing house in the U.S. thought it would be better for its marketing. In the original, the Spanish title was *Del Buen Salvaje al Buen Revolucionario*, and in the French, Italian, Portuguese and other nearly twenty translations the title was closer to that original one, which associates Rousseau's *bon sauvage* concept to the idealized notion of the revolutionary guerrilla fighter.

My father's book debunked the myth of the "noble fighter" standing against social injustice, the underdog against the oppressive establishment around him. This is a concept pervasive in Latin America and personi-fied in an idealized image of Ernesto "Che" Guevara; for some Western ideologues, a concept identified with the so-called "freedom fighter." The book went on further to suggest that this romantic myth of the noble freedom fighter as a social hero represented a skewed political posturing and generated a pernicious populism that tended to blame outside factors for Latin American society's own failings. The U.S. title made the clear point of underscoring that the book contained ideas related to the rift in understanding that lies beneath the Latin America-U.S. relationship and originating in this misapplied myth of the noble savage, transformed into noble revolutionary.

My father died a year before the Berlin wall came down. Witnessing the accelerating cascade of events that led to the tearing down of that

The author's father, Carlos Rangel, and his second wife, Sofia Imber,
interviewing former President Carter in 1986

Source: Uncredited Photo, as appeared in "Marx y Los Socialismos Reales y Otros
Ensayos" (Rangel 1989)

wall would have been a great satisfaction for him, as he was very much
against the repressive regimes that, led by Russia, had made communism
a new method of subjugation by tyrants, using as their excuse slogans
such as "people's power," "revolution" and "anti-imperialism."

Through him, I had the opportunity to personally meet four presidents
and several major political figures in Venezuela, as well as many ambas-
sadors, powerbrokers, and major corporate figures. By a logistical mishap,
I missed meeting former President Jimmy Carter, the first U.S. president
that I had a chance to vote for and whom I never had the chance to thank
for the warm condolences sent to our family upon my father's death.

The opportunity of knowing these people gave me a special insight
into the influence of politics and political discourses in daily life, and a
special interest in understanding and interpreting the value of politicians'
work, their passion and motivation for service, as well as the nuances
of politicians' power and machinery, demagoguery, and self-interest.
I do believe in the worth of professional politicians and in their value
to the community. I do believe that a politician's fundamental job is to

lead coalitions dedicated to the improvement of her or his community's welfare. I do believe that a politician's role is to understand key issues and how they affect their constituencies, to determine stakeholders, to establish a position on key issues, and to lead his or her coalitions into formulating and implementing policies in favor of the position that he or she has adopted.

President Bill Clinton was the ultimate professional politician. He created coalitions and established majorities for issues as diverse as welfare reform, NAFTA, and a war in which he protected the Muslims against the Christians in Bosnia. During his presidency, he was a politician engaged in his craft, and he embraced that fact with such a relish and sense of social purpose that it seemed to override his self-interest. I voted for Bill Clinton, twice.

I am a natural born American: a U.S. citizen born abroad from an American parent. As such, I have all the rights and privileges of anyone born in America, including the ultimate right of running for president of the U.S.,[1] and yet, in Venezuela, and given my family background, I was engaged in the political process. I worked at polling booths and was an "electoral witness." I was there on February 4 1991 when Col. Hugo Chávez tried to violently overthrow the government of President Carlos Andrés Pérez (for whom I also voted). I witnessed then the preview of things to come: the politicking, the demagoguery, and the divisive reaction from the Venezuelan body politic. The situation made it clear to me how divisive self-interest could trump the possibility of moving a country institutionally towards a better society. This was what made me decide to return for good to the U.S., where my wife was working on her Ph.D. at UCLA. I wrapped up my MBA at UCLA (with an emphasis on economics), and worked for fifteen years in businesses related to Latin America.[2]

I have had the opportunity to see opulence and extreme poverty up close, and class and other social barriers in pernicious operation. I have seen the enormous difference on the ground between civically driven political actions and ideologically driven political demagoguery. My upbringing makes me believe in moral rectitude and the existence of moral values and yet, also to understand human failings and second chances. I embrace the idea that we can strive towards a better future by learning from mistakes in the past, and that the future can include improved opportunities for those presently disenfranchised, an opportunity that includes living in a society that cares about the failings and failures, and the virtues and successes of all its members. If my upbringing, what I have learned from these observations and the idea of a possible better future for all in civilized society founded on our constitutional principles makes me a "liberal," so be it.

Not a Baby Boomer Anymore

May 22, 2008

William Jefferson Clinton was the first baby boomer U.S. president. Many of us identified with him because we had lived what he had lived: the anguish of Vietnam, dabbling with musical instruments, experimenting with lifestyles, living with The Beatles, The Doors, Three Dog Night, Joni Mitchell, and The Band, switching from black and white to color television, the Apollo Program, *The Whole Earth Catalog* and *The Silent Spring*, the long, hot summers, mourning the Kennedys and MLK… the baby boomer gestalt experience.

Now comes Senator Barack Hussein Obama and, with him, an interesting milestone: for many of us he will be the first person we vote for president who is younger than ourselves.[3] How will his potential tenure be affected as he becomes the first post-baby boom president? How does he relate to the growing angst of baby boomer retirement? What does retirement mean today for most of us? How does social security play into this? How will health care be taken care of? And to what extent will he empathize with the baby boomer social activism that still affects our consciousness and lives?

Spam and Potatoes

Some of us remember the price/wage freeze solutions of Nixon and Carter, and are concerned with the return of high inflation. We incredulously look at inflation reports today that tell us that "seasonally adjusted" gas prices have been low over the last few months (Andron 2008, Hernandez 2008), even though the pump indicates close to $4.00 a gallon[4]; we skeptically read that unemployment rates are historically low[5]; we clearly see food prices go up, meat giving way to Spam[6] in many households. Truly, government statistics are not what they used to be.

As baby boomers, we now find ourselves living this new economic reality while squeezed in the middle of three generations. Changes in the social net that have brought about hyper-nuclear families in geographical dispersion have made it more difficult to create family support networks. We have tried to compensate with advances in transportation and communication infrastructure, bringing down the cost of travel and allowing us to be in "remote" touch and "virtual" availability (DeMocker

2008). But as our parents and we ourselves age, we are less capable of maintaining a real support network for our less able parents. Diminished opportunities for baby boomers create hardships on their parents, and guilt and bitterness all around.

The pain and effort of trying to deal with our senior generation, coping with the challenge of our own generation, and trying to establish a future for our relay generation poses challenges for baby boomers that are unresolved in our social support network. Our senior generation needs us: with a social support network that is increasingly lacking after years of hard work, our parents require increasing care, which we are willing to give, but which becomes more and more difficult to do. Our children count on us: the rising cost of college education absorbs all possible extra income, yet we still hope to give to our children the opportunity of having a higher education, at least at the same level that we had. The structural costs within the university systems absorb all subsidies, grants and financial support programs devised to help us afford our children's education. Furthermore, adding to our frustration is the fact that as education becomes more expensive, its value diminishes. When we graduated from college, it was a privilege to do so and it gave us a real start in the marketplace. Nowadays, a college education is just a minimum requirement for many, just as high school was when we graduated. For voting baby boomers, this squeeze in the middle and our own anxieties over having a secure future are top-of-mind concerns.

Bleeding-Heart-Liberals are People Too

In addition to these anxieties, baby boomers may wonder whether the lessons from the Long Hot Summers, Vietnam, and the Imperial Presidency are still remembered. The Vietnam connection to our present is very strong. Besides its ideological scars on our psyche, we look back at that era and see that some unfortunate political and economic lessons seem to have been unlearned. It is troubling that the dots connecting gigantic deficits, the structurally weak dollar, the expected price of oil and the cost of the war are being overlooked. Nearly 60,000 Americans died and more than 300,000 were wounded and the lessons are being forgotten, even though their blood sacrifice is clearly the most controversial of all that America has undertaken and spilled. The ideological causes behind the U.S. involvement in Vietnam are still arguable. The war tactics and strategies used there are still questioned. The true, final geopolitical outcome is still not clear, and certainly did not reflect the "Domino Theory" prevalent at the time. Did we learn anything from the Vietnam experience? Have we forgotten everything that we learned?

The economic consequences of Vietnam contributed to major stagflation in the 1970s and, undoubtedly, to a lesser standing of the U.S. among the community of nations. Politically within the U.S., the arrogance of the Hawks and the self-righteousness of the Doves divided the country, spawning the first ideologically driven urban unrest in more than fifty years as well as deadly urban and campus protests. These troubled times tempered the electorate and led to what were to be later known as the "Reagan Democrats" who elected Carter, Reagan, and Clinton. These times then rolled into a Western-Southern populist coalition wave from the late 1970s to the late 1990s; a wave that broke with a surge of true libertarian conservative values that, at first, united the country but now is increasingly divisive by its ideological imposition of sectarian personal values through political manipulation.

There is now a wave rolling similar to the one originated by Vietnam but this time, instead of being driven by that combination of libertarian and conservative values, it seems to be driven by a new combination of libertarian and humanitarian values.[7] Baby boomers lived this history already, and some can see it. Senator Obama has a family history adrift in these baby boomer currents. Let us hope Senator Obama has learned this history and can ride the wave.

The Terrorists Have Won... So Far

June 1, 2008

I remember as a young man talking about terrorism with my father and what it meant. The word says it all: it is about terror—putting terror in the mind of the victims. The objective is to disrupt society, to make ordinary life a life on the edge, always expecting the unthinkable to happen. This disruption of civil life is expected to result in a disruption of civil liberties and a breakdown of civil institutions. The anarchists of the early 1900s believed that with their terrorist actions they would force the government to react repressively against its own people. The people in turn would react against repression and overthrow the government. George Santayana famously said it: "Those who cannot remember the past are condemned to repeat it." Unfortunately, that now seems to be the case with our current strategy on terrorism—with a twist.

In America today, repeated breaches against civil liberties and basic constitutional freedoms are excused by 9/11 The campaigning that suggests that anything but unwavering support to these breaches is a "9/10 mentality" or is "soft on terrorism" is a trick to polarize positions in this regard, make it a black or white issue, an either/or situation. This situation does not lend itself to a clear cut *anti* or *pro* position on measures taken by the government. Whereas it is true that before the horrendous surprise attack on innocent civilians in September of 2001 the American intelligence and defense apparatus was apparently unaware or dismissive of the growing terrorism threat, the fact is that we do not seem to be better off now, which should be the goal of any antiterrorist measures. Instability in our world seems to have always been tied to the price of oil, and if that is any indicator, we are living unstable times.[8] Al-Qaeda seems stronger than ever in Pakistan, possibly threatening India, and growing in influence and size in the lawless areas of southern Sudan, Central Africa, and Somalia. The Latin American terrorist group FARC (Fuerzas Armadas Revolucionarias de Colombia) is possibly networking with Iran, and certainly trying aggressively to obtain materials for radioactive weapons (Bachelet 2008).[9]

The strong-handed tactics America has used internationally to "fight terrorism" have created new motivation for our enemies, new training fields (including Gitmo) and more, instead of fewer, terrorist foot soldiers with a passionate hate for America. By using "extraordinary rendition" and off territory prisons, openly skirting international torture prohibitions and Habeas Corpus, the government has undermined our own capacity to legally eliminate terrorist activity. The clear example is Omar Abdel-Rahman (the blind sheik) and many of his associates, who were arrested, judged, and are currently in jail for plotting and bombing the World Trade Center in 1995. In a well-documented trial within the justice system of the American courts, they were charged, tried, and convicted. They have now been taken out from the terrorist networks. The detainees at Guantanamo are there, sometimes for the right reason (for example—Khalid Sheikh Mohammed), and sometimes for the wrong ones. The real problem is that we do not know which is which. Of the thousands of "terrorists" that have passed through Gitmo, only one (as I write this) has actually been brought to trial and sentenced (through a plea deal).[10] Fewer than twenty have been charged officially with any crime. The vast majority has been repatriated, either with no further explanation, or to a regime that has kept them imprisoned with no further charges except the suspicion that they are terrorists. Many return to a broken life, embittered by the experience and after having interacted with true terrorists. Now they have a real reason to be part of "the worst of the worst" criminal terrorist networks.

The promise of rule of law, civil protections, representative democracy, and respect for human rights has been undermined by our current policies for combating terrorism. The core premises of what makes our civil society have been pushed aside, creating the conditions for more terrorism as a reaction to such uncivil tactics. *In other words: the terrorists are winning.* The political anarchist of the past has delved into the modern religious terrorist.

The definition of winning when combating terrorism needs to change, and the McCain path is not the one. Winning for America is not a situation in which everything our society is about is destroyed in order to create a false sense of security with repressive measures. Winning for America is not a situation in which more terrorists are created than eliminated. Winning for America is not a situation that creates more international isolation from our allies, more distance from our friends, and that dismisses as weak the view that seeks to regain our moral standing, the view which—in the end—will be the only true way to combat terrorism from its roots.

And Justice for All

June 2, 2008

To judge is to secure all relevant facts pertaining to a situation at hand and, by the use of reason, come to a conclusion regarding the situation. When the situation involves a dispute between parties, an independent arbiter of the facts can resolve that dispute in a fair manner. When the dispute is between an individual and society, this independent arbiter judges and resolves according to the rules of society. In order to avoid arbitrary application, the rules of society are established independently of the judges that apply them. Judges must abide by these rules, guidelines, and laws to ensure fairness. The laws themselves are written based upon a commonly accepted set of principles deemed to be immutable, yet subject to interpretation. In our case, the laws are primarily based on the Constitution's Bill of Rights and subsequent amendments. Laws, however, are written under the constraints of bounded rationality,[11] and when confronted with a dispute a judge should be able to consider all the facts of the situation and, utilizing reasoned discretion, interpret the intent of the law to impart justice—in all its platonic meaning. Misdirected judicial discretion is best checked by the appellate process, not by political posturing and election slogans.

Moral certitude and moral relativism have been in a deadlock fight since the time of Plato's Republic, and perhaps before. The belief that there is an immutable essence of true justice and that we must create a model of that "platonic" essence, devoid of any extraneous influence, is critical in the framework of a judicial system believed to be fair. If such a model were in fact enacted as "the law of the land" by those designated by our framers, then no question should arise in the interpretation of such law. By this strict interpretation, application of the law would be just and fair, universal and timeless.

"War on drugs," "war on terrorism," and "law and order" political ideologues have viewed the discretionary interpretation of laws by judges in the context of what has been described as a fear of tyranny: a fear of the arbitrary and dehumanizing exercise of power by activist judges.[12] That is why, as legislators, these ideologues have passed and enacted formulaic laws that seek to remove judicial discretion. These laws include mandatory sentencing, and "three strikes you're out" laws, that come close to skirting the Eighth Amendment clause on cruel and unusual punishment and the Fourteenth Amendment provision for equal protection under the law. Internationally, our government has "found" ways to skirt Habeas Corpus and sought to redefine torture, in order to apply a misdirected sense of personal justice and revenge that does not stand the test of civilized society and rule of law. Domestically, this frame of mind reverts into the unintended consequences of the war on drugs removing judicial discretion by enacting mandatory sentencing guidelines which contravene equal protection and fair punishment. The misdirection of resources that these policies mandate fail to address the core issues regarding drug abuse, leading to growing rates of incarceration as well as a failure to effectively curb international drug trafficking and its concomitant terrorism and violence.

It is in that sense that so called "constructivist" judges would apply the law as written, as opposed to the interpretation of such law relative to a situation. As it is, however, when laws are written, bounded rationality exists and the essence of true justice will inevitably escape the best intentioned lawmaker attempting prescriptive laws. The consequences of trying to be absolutely prescriptive when writing laws can thus have as a consequence a miscarriage of the essence of justice, and in fact it is an encroachment of the branches of power as the legislative usurps duties and responsibilities of the judiciary.

It is when restrained by prescriptive legislation that judges, and by extension our society, will in fact fail to exercise a model of the essence of justice in the courtroom. For example, if a person steals a slice of pizza he could serve a penalty of years in prison, if it were his "third strike," regardless of any attenuating circumstances. Faced with such prospect, some prosecutors or judges may be unwilling to pursue or willing to dismiss such a case, leading to a loss for society, as a crime goes unpunished. In most cases, however, and contrary to principles of "the punishment should fit the crime" and the expectation of rehabilitation, that person will be locked away. In California for thirty years, no parole, for punching someone in a barroom brawl, bouncing a check, and shoplifting, for example; antisocial behavior, yes, but not exactly *"Lockdown: Raw"* material.[13]

The consequence of mandatory sentencing, in particular as it relates to incarceration, has been a growth rate greater than the population growth, leading the U.S. to be the country with the highest incarceration rate in the world, with 1 in 100 adults currently under the jurisdiction of the federal, state or local penitentiary system. Of these, nearly 20 percent are in state or local prison for drug related charges as their major offense, that is, not classified as violent offenders (murder, assault, robbery), property offenders (burglary, vandalism, etc.) or weapons charges, all of these charges sometimes associated with drug offenders. Some of those charged with drug offenses are dealers and should be in jail, but the vast majority consists of users in need of treatment. Most of the small and middle-level dealers in state prison probably are in fact charged with other major offenses such as those listed before. Persons held in federal custody under drug charges account for over 53 percent of the federal total, most of them the notorious drug lords of lore. Federal prisoners make up approximately 12.5 percent of all prisoners in the U.S. (U.S. Department of Justice 2008).[14]

Crimes against property and persons deserve jail time. Crimes related to behavior deserve punishment. Antisocial behavior deserves punishment and sometimes prison. Self-destructive behavior requires treatment. In a DUI it is the driving that gets punished, not the influence. If an intoxicated person takes a bus home, he is not arrested, as the behavior may be self-destructive, but is not overtly antisocial. If an officer of the law boards the bus and approaches the intoxicated person and determines he is "just a harmless drunk" the officer may let such drunkard go on his way. If, on the other hand, the intoxication is drug induced, the intoxicated person may be arrested and end up in prison on drug charges, adding to the growing percentage of mandatory incarcerated people in the U.S.

It used to be that people with mental infirmities were locked away in the attic or in an "insane asylum." We have come a long way and have recognized the inhumanity of such solutions, improving treatment and institutionalization procedures for the mentally ill. A great amount of research is dedicated to determine the best ways to treat such problems; yet the behavioral and personality problems associated with drug abuse are not best treated in prison. Taxpayer investment resources are squandered sending drug abusers and addicts away to bigger and newer prisons, instead of determining better rehabilitation methods for them. The prisons become revolving doors that drive these users into more antisocial behavior, and the existing drug rehab centers do not fare much better, with dismal success rates. It is a moral imperative that we learn how to treat and control the use and abuse of psychotropic drugs and drug addiction. A successful response to this imperative has worldwide consequences, reaching directly into Mexico, Colombia, Afghanistan, and other countries, impacting violent crime here and in drug producing territories, and associated with the success of various terrorist groups. Our drug problem affects our international policies and relations. Right now we are not even close to an adequate response.[15]

It is unfortunate that under the cover of a mantle of moral certitude, legislators abusing mandatory sentencing have taken away from the judiciary the capacity to judge what action best befits each situation, and what punishment fits each crime. A thorough review is required of this legacy of the war on drugs, a legacy that, with its populist calls of being "tough on crime" or decrying "moral relativism," blinds us to real solutions to the problem and fails to address its link with terrorism. This is a legacy that is currently blocking the promise of the pursuit of a better society with compassion, fairness and justice for all.

Notes

1.   Natural citizenship rights are entitled to children born abroad, from an American citizen parent that happened to be abroad, even if that means that they are dual citizens. Full U.S. citizenship rights are bestowed, exactly as if the child had been born on U.S. soil. That child is considered a natural-born American, as natural as those born in U.S. territory. This is a corollary to the fact that, constitutionally, anyone born in the U.S. or its territories is a U.S. citizen, regardless of the citizenship or immigration status of the child's parents. The relevant regulation, as published in the U.S. Department of State's website is stated in legalese as: *Acquisition of US Citizenship by a Child Born Abroad - Birth Abroad to One Citizen and One Alien Parent in Wedlock: A child born abroad to one U.S. citizen parent and one alien parent acquires U.S. citizenship at birth under Section 301(g) INA provided the citizen parent was physically present in the U.S. for the time period required by the law applicable at the time of the child's birth.*

Regulations on dual citizenship vary by the countries that are involved and the applicable law at the time of birth. I am a dual citizen as allowed by both my countries and can technically run for office in either, albeit having to renounce to the other if doing so. Senator Obama, having been born to a Kenyan citizen living abroad, had dual-citizen status and had to choose at age twenty-one by Kenyan law. He chose to embrace America as his country of citizenship. His father was a dual citizen from Kenya and the U.K. Senator McCain's status is unquestionable, as he was born in a U.S. territory at the time (Panama's Canal Zone) and of American parents (similar to Barry Goldwater, born in what then was a territory, Arizona). In the past, President Chester Arthur is said to have been born in Canada of an American mother. Lowell Weicker (senator from Connecticut and presidential primary candidate, 1980) was born in Paris, and George Romney (presidential primary candidate, 1968 and father of Governor Mitt Romney) was born in Mexico.

2.   I now have a small business of my own, and have run it over the last six years. Political re-engagement has been a long time coming. Senator Barack Obama's candidacy motivated me, once again, to communicate and to engage in the political process in order to contribute, even by just a little, with the improvement of my community.

3.   An interesting phenomenon, repeated throughout the U.S., was also true in my case: my mother, myself and my daughter, all voted for Senator Obama; three generations in synch.

4.   In citing Merrill Lynch indices and unnamed investors, Sandra Hernandez (2008) states: "the consumer price index downplays the 39 percent increase in gasoline and a 133 percent rise in corn in the past year."

5.   Dana Perino, White House briefing of June 6, 2008: "We're obviously not happy with the unemployment number that had gone up. We do think it was in line with the expectations for the current economy, and we do also believe that it's important to look at a couple of things. One, the number in large part was increased by new job applicants, and it usually takes new job applicants a little while longer to find work. So while it's a concern that the unemployment rate jumped to 5.5 percent, that is still historically low, and lower than the averages of the '70s, '80s and '90s." (As published on the White House website, www.whitehouse.gov, Press Briefings section)

6.   As reported in the *San Francisco Chronicle* on May 29, 2008 (*Tough Economy Demands Spam*): "Spam's maker, Hormel Foods Corp., reported last week that it saw strong sales of Spam in the second quarter, helping push up its profits 14 percent. According to sales information coming from Hormel, provided by the Nielsen Co., Spam sales were up 10.6 percent in the 12-week period ending May 3, compared with last year. In the last 24 weeks, sales were up nearly 9 percent" (Fredrix 2008).

7.   This notion of libertarian/humanist driven values perhaps was taken mainstream with GW Bush's appealing campaign slogans in 2000 calling for "Compassionate Conservative" ideals and the claim that he represented such ideals. The concept itself has been developing at least since the late 1970s according to Wikipedia's dictionary entry for the term.

8.   At the time of this writing, the price of oil was heading towards record heights close to $150 a barrel. At this level, countries such as Iran, Russia, and Venezuela have excess resources that they use to extend their influence around the world.

9.   "The State Department said Thursday it was 'deeply concerned' by reports that a Colombian guerrilla group possessed presumed depleted uranium, which experts say poses little threat but could indicate a push to get something more dangerous. 'We are deeply concerned by the reports that FARC members were trafficking in uranium,' State Department spokeswoman Heide Bronke Fulton said. 'This

underscores the terrorist threat that FARC poses to the people of Colombia and to the region.'" (Bachelet 2008).

10. David Hicks, a Muslim convert originally from Australia was convicted through a plea deal in late March 2008. The deal was for seven years, with time after nine months suspended, effectively setting him free almost as soon as he landed in Australia on May 29, 2008. As part of the deal he was not to speak to the media for a year, not get any money for his story, and not sue the U.S. government, as well as withdraw any allegations that he was mistreated or tortured.

11. Bounded Rationality is a concept that addresses decision making under the intellectual constraint of man's cognitive limitations for finding and analyzing all possible variables and scenarios to a given set of problems, and all the implications of such decisions. This constraint "binds" reasoning and leads to "satisficing" solutions; solutions that while may not be optimal, satisfy all known factors in the decision (Simon 1991).

12. Gregory S. Alexander (1985), in a review of "Reconstructing American Law" by Bruce A. Ackerman, writes: "The Constructivist fears that if we rely on non-rationalist intuitionism in the welfare state, discretion in the hands of bureaucrats inevitably will degenerate into the arbitrary and dehumanizing exercise of power. Constructivism self-consciously formalizes legal analysis on the basis of the traditional rationalist belief that without rules we lack the 'cognitive control' essential to prevent oppression and social injustice. Ackerman's call to make legal analysis more formal, rigorous, and professional grows out of the belief, or hope, that the right conceptions of reason and justice in law, systematically determined as some mixture of efficiency and fairness, will shield us against 'tyranny.'"

13. This refers to the sensationalist *Lockdown: Raw* TV Show on *MSNBC* depicting violent criminals in jail. It is said that the rate of "capture" is somewhere between 100 to 400 times the rate of offense, that is someone will be caught committing a traffic offense, for example, only if they frequently commit traffic offenses. Consequently it is repeated criminal behavior that leads to the capture and conviction of the criminal. So, in the example in the text, the person may have acted antisocially perhaps 600 times or maybe only three times before actually appearing before a court of law three times. This is where attenuating circumstances and judicial discretion come into play. By stuffing prisons with non-violent offenders we create a system that, due to overcrowding, forces the release or early release of violent people that should remain in jail.

14. For the most recent breakdown of incarceration statistics see Bureau of Justice Statistics Bulletin, December 2008; US Department of Justice, Office of Justice Programs, Pub. NCJ 224280 (U.S. Department of Justice 2008).

15. After I wrote this essay, there was an interesting in-depth article appeared in *Los Angeles Times* on the successes and failures of drug rehab centers in the U.S. (Roan 2008).

6

The National Campaign (Finally) Begins

Coronation Night: A New Beginning

June 3, 2008

After months of anticipation building, today Tuesday June 3, the final day of the primaries, the media is in a frenzy. As I was having lunch, eating beef tattaki—a kind of raw meat—the TV in the restaurant was on. When I sat down, the CNN ticker said that Senator Obama had 1,983 delegates out of 2,118 needed for the nomination. When the food was served—fairly quickly I may add—the ticker had changed to 1,985. I was unsure, wondering if I had seen the number wrong before. As I finished lunch, paying attention now, the ticker number said 1,986. By the time I got home that evening, the ticker said 2,012 on one channel, 2,129 on another, and 2,007 on the third, before any real votes had been counted. All cable news channels were on continuous coverage of what they dubbed "Coronation Night." It was quite instructive, with all three major political figures of the moment giving back-to-back speeches.[1] The obvious mathematical inevitability was there for all to see now, in cold numbers. The primaries had come to an end and by the end of the night Senator Obama had been declared the presumptive nominee of the Democratic Party for the 2008 elections. The great question on everybody's mind now is: what will Senator Clinton do? The buzz in the media is the "dream ticket" of Obama-Clinton. Why would she want that? Why would he want that?

Her supporters may think that this is the next best thing for her, but it really is not. Analyzing strategically the office of the VP in terms of its political influence and legacy, this is not an office for someone wanting to build a future and make history. Over the last sixty years, there have been few instances that would make a case for convincing an ambitious and politically savvy person that being VP of the U.S. is the second best thing to being the president. Incumbent vice presidents who were elected to the presidency are very few, though many attempted: the presidency was thrust upon Truman, Johnson, and Ford, and Ford was not even re-elected—and holds the distinction of being the only president that was not elected to the executive branch. Alben Barkley lost the nomination to Adlai Stevenson, Nixon failed in his first attempt, as incumbent VP, to be elected; Hubert Humphrey lost; Walter Mondale lost (though he was not the incumbent at the time); George H. Bush won on Reagan's momentum, and, like Ford, could not get reelected; and what can we say about Dan Quayle?; or Al Gore... well, in *his* case it is complicated. In other words, out of all presidents and vice presidents since 1939, only one incumbent VP (George H. W. Bush) has actually won the presidency in an election. It is a dire record for the VP office position and someone wanting to consolidate political power from it.

So what may be the best way to channel the political energy created by senators Obama and Clinton during this primary season? Why waste that energy in a VP slot? Should Senator Clinton really use that voter energy for an appointed executive branch position? Would that be a better legacy?

It seems clear, when analyzing the situation, that she has the chance now of becoming an even greater force in the American political landscape, but the vice presidency is not the way to go. Her position as senator from New York is secure for years to come and she should not give it up. This is not a term-limited position, and the combination of national political power with eventual seniority could make her one of, if not the most powerful senator in U.S. history.[2]

By not squandering her political power at this time, but managing it in order to strengthen the potential Democratic victory in November, she can succeed in reaching the policy goals she campaigned for. Her most powerful position will be as a de facto liaison between the legislative and executive branch, something she did before in her years in the White House, but can now do more overtly, in designated, currently non-existing formalized roles. Working committees and task forces dedicated to health care in particular, for example, could in effect be led by her, combining the efforts of two branches of government with a sense of urgency to get things done. We cannot afford as a nation to lose her now to the vice presidency.

Regarding the vice presidency itself, the Republican Party and all its pundits would love to know who goes on the Democratic ticket as soon as possible. With the Republican Convention in St. Paul after the Democratic Convention in Denver, it is to their advantage to quickly know who the Democratic vice presidential candidate is. Not only can they attack more than one candidate, they can counterbalance with their own VP candidate. The pressure must be shifted to the Republicans regarding VP choices, as Senator McCain has to compensate for his weaknesses as a candidate very quickly. Senator Obama's best strategy right now (and the Democratic Party's) is to put off any public announcement of his choice for as long as he can.

The End is Near

September 1 , 2008

As all signs point to the beginning of the end, the media and message clutter increases, distracting from core issues. Clearly the endgame centers on voters entrusting the government of the nation to one of the two contending teams. The breakdown of this simple concept into issue-driven topics can confuse the overarching concept of government and its role in modern society. Seeking the hottest issue—is it energy? is it the war? is it the economy?—or the "gotcha" button: is her daughter pregnant? Was he in the Church?—will continue, in reality, to distract from the core of each voter's decision on Tuesday November 4, a decision that will affect directly the lives of all of us. As pundits seek to find the issue that answers the "what's in it for me" question, or find the closeted skeleton that brings on a gag reflex, the voters—hopefully—will still retain a sense of perspective.

There is no doubt that running a government is a complex task, entrenched in bureaucratic rules, entitlement programs, general organizational inertia, and extremely small amounts of truly discretionary resources. Puny mortals confront this complex task and, although it may seem that their effect is little, it really is not. That is why it is critical to have capable leadership, effective judgment, clear thinking, and sound policy goals in the minds of top government elected officials. Of course, government makes a difference. If you doubt it, just look at the last eight years. The last eight years have seen increasing government intervention and intrusion into the private life of citizens, while at the same time decreasing government regulation on what should matter, trashing the economy, and destroying our reputation abroad.

Senator Obama is "lucky." He is lucky that he had to work so hard for the nomination, tempering him and his team, showcasing him frequently; he is lucky to have had Senator Clinton as a worthy contender. The attack points he was most vulnerable on are still out there but have been somewhat overcome: the inexperience argument, the unknown factor, the difference wedge issue, his unseemly acquaintances, and his weakness in fighting have been either effectively deflected by his team or ineffectively used by Senator McCain's team. The long primary campaign allowed the Obama team to clear out these attack points early. It is now time to focus on the end game: reiterating Barack Obama's capacity for leadership and judgment.

The only caveat to this approach—the proper image to portray now—is the potential return to a characterization of Obama as the aloof, elitist, and detached persona portrayed by his opponents at the beginning of the campaign. The inclusion of Senator Biden as the VP candidate, the "makeover" of Mrs. Obama, and the (expected) intense participation of the Clintons in the campaign will go a very long way in deflecting this resurgent attack, telegraphed early by the opposing camp with the selection of Governor Palin as Senator McCain's running mate.

The Electoral College strategy must not be overlooked at this time either, with the battle focused on the Rustbelt and Florida, maybe Georgia and Virginia, and mobilizing Western regions as well. The Northeast seems secure, as well as Illinois and the West Coast, but these states cannot be neglected, obviously. Alaska is gone, and probably Louisiana (on account of hurricane Gustav and Governor Bobby Jindal), as well as Texas, obviously. Current readings of polls give Senator Obama the edge in the College, but the final combination that will allow him to gain the trust of the voters and become the next president of the United States is the one that showcases once again his capable judgment and leadership on the issues, and the "one of us/common values" message that Senator Biden, Michelle, and the Clintons can establish effectively in the battleground regions.[3]

Governor Sarah Palin: The Choice

September 4, 2008

Some things seem clichéd and redundant until highlighted by contrast. It is said that the first real presidential decision a candidate makes is the choice of running mate: the vice president. Senator Obama's and Senator McCain's choices allow us to understand the political mind and process that each one uses to make fundamental government decisions, decisions that affect the way the country will be run. It is by all means true that the person entrusted as the vice president shapes the job, and it has been remarkable the extent to which this position has changed under the Bush/Cheney administration. The vice presidential office has come a long way from being what John Adams described—while serving as the first U.S. vice president—"the most insignificant office that ever the invention of man contrived or his imagination conceived."[4]

In addition to constitutional duties as the president's emergency successor and president of the Senate, currently the vice president is customarily a participant in cabinet meetings and, by Congressional fiat, a member of the National Security Council. It should be pointed out that the Twenty-Fifth Amendment also gives the VP the responsibility—in joint action along with a simple majority of the cabinet—to declare the president unable or unfit to discharge his/her duties at any given time, a potentially significant issue given Senator McCain's age as well as his repeated cancer treatments. The actual political clout of the VP is of course made by the person in the position but real duties, both customary and constitutional, make the selection a critical one for the shaping of the government.

The case for Sarah Palin as VP from a governmental view is hard to make, but is understandable from a political view. Yes, she is an interesting woman whom I had noticed before her new position in the limelight, when news accounts of Trig Palin's birth on April 18, 2008 circulated. It was remarkable at the time to read how she combined her personal life while successfully managing the highest elected office of her state. She has what they now call "a compelling story." She has the potential to become a political figure of stature, and certainly the spotlight of her candidacy will help her in this. Standing now in the limelight we can see her better. She clearly passes the core or "litmus test" issues for die-hard republicans: She is pro-life, an NRA member, a practicing Christian and, among other things, a proponent of creationism as an alternative theory to evolution. She is also an advocate of drilling in the ANWR and a believer that global warming has nothing to do with man's activities. You cannot get much more core Republican than that![5] Except—she did raise taxes on the oil companies.

Alaska is the largest state in geographical territory and one with the smallest population—about a third of that of Broward County, Florida, or about the same as that of Ft. Worth, Texas—and has a state budget approximately twice the size of Chicago's and a third in size of Los Angeles', driven by taxable revenues on the oil industry. A bit of a populist, Governor Palin has regularly given money to Alaska citizens, taking it from windfall profit taxes on oil companies, and she changed her original position on "The Bridge to Nowhere" only after it was clear that no more federal funding would be available and Alaskans would have to pay for its completion. This apparent parochial streak seems to run a bit deep in her, understandably, given her local political environment. Perhaps, since all politics are local, having one of the most parochial of politicians we have seen in a long time thrust to the national spotlight makes some perverse sense.

Not only does she seem to have taken great advantage of "earmarks" for her local constituency, her record could be a textbook case of small politicking within a small community. In such a small state as that of Alaska (in population, not territory) it is obvious that most people in public office may be somehow connected with each other and with the region's main economic interests—the oil companies. That, however, makes for a very different kind of governance—one primarily based on insider rules—than the governance which will be asked from her as vice president of the U.S.

Governor Palin's record, as much as has been revealed, demonstrates a streak of obsessive control based on views and moral values which are not mainstream. She is definitely not someone you want to have on the other side if you live in a small town, not even if you are her mother-in-law—who is rumored to have tried to succeed her as mayor of Wasilla and failed because Governor Palin did not agree with her views on abortion.[6] We have seen the harsh imposition of personal views upon organizations and societies before, and she certainly does not seem to be, or have a record as, the conciliatory type, the kind of person that reaches across the aisle. She seems more the kind of person that runs a two-way conversation one way. At a time when bipartisanship, conciliation, and unity are critical to improve the future life of all Americans, Governor Palin personifies a combination of President Bush and Vice President Cheney at its worst (albeit prepped by closet Roves). Her acceptance speech stressed and seemed to cherish that view. Her between-the-lines script was: "*I am a tough regular guy and I do things my way—you better don't mess with me.*"

The most significant personal event in her life may have been the recent birth of her son Trig, afflicted with Down's syndrome. In statements regarding this event, she clearly ratifies her pro-life position. The commitment a parent and their families need to make in order to provide a loving, happy and fulfilling life to a child born with disabilities is substantial, and Governor Palin is fortunate enough to be able to fulfill that commitment, and to be able to make that choice. It is unfortunate that not everyone in our society has that capability, however. By taking away that choice, the anti-abortion movement would force parents and families to make commitments that they may be unable to fulfill, particularly given the state of our health care system, especially regarding chronic conditions. Governor Palin's position on abortion as only allowable if the mother's life is in danger, if it were implemented, places pregnant women in danger. When faced with personal or medical dilemmas of the sort that Governor Palin had, some would choose not to have their baby—and resort to unsafe or criminal actions if abortion were to be made illegal. Governor Palin is in fact the epitome of what pro-choice is all about: she was able to choose to have her son, and she is to be commended for that.

As I stated, Sarah Palin is a politician of note, particularly because of her work ethic and her integrity in her beliefs. She comes across as a well-intentioned and opinionated person, with a certain folksy bent, and a disdain for the opposition. She has merit, but the more we learn about her and her character traits, the more I worry about the possibility of her being the vice president of the United States—and even more so of becoming the president.

The choice of the VP candidate is the first executive decision of a potential president and a reflection of that presidential candidate's character and judgment—as well as his political savvy. It seems that Senator McCain failed this test. Given the months that Senator McCain had for making an inspired choice (since January), his choice is unimpressive. It does not seem to have been based on the soundest of reasons. Senator McCain's decision seems deeply steeped in presidential politics and from a certain impulsive trait (a "maverick" choice?); it seems motivated by one single goal: to win the election. Senator Obama's VP choice, in contrast, appears driven by the purpose of running the government of the United States. Senator McCain has demonstrated with this and his other actions that he wants to be *elected* president of the United States. Senator Obama has demonstrated that he wants to *be* president of the United States.

The Emperor's New Clothes

September 7, 2008

Senator McCain represents the Republican Party. The Republican Party stands for staying the course. President Bush and Vice President Cheney have focused on maintaining what amounts to increasing government intrusion into citizen's private lives, increasing regulations and restrictions, kowtowing to big business interests, and concentrating power in the Presidency. In spite of claims made to the contrary by his campaign, Senator McCain stands for continuity of the current government.

The Legacy

Over the last eight years we have seen civil liberties eroded in the name of patriotism, independent scientific thought ridiculed and expunged from official documentation, and the Constitution's Bill of Rights attacked, reinterpreted, or simply ignored. When challenged or rebuked in court for its actions, the administration has called for replacing judges that rule against their ideology with "constructivist" judges (while decrying judicial activism at the same time). We have seen a new plethora of hardships thrown upon individuals and small businesses, from decreased social benefits, decreased mid- and higher-education supports and increased financial burdens, to Small Business Administration disincentives and modified bankruptcy laws while protecting and serving big business, for example by eroding whistleblower protections. At the same time, we have seen licensing and waivers allowing market concentration for big business, for example in the energy, health care and telecommunications industries, turning a blind eye to corporate mismanagement of regulatory basics (leading to the financial crisis), or awarding contracts to well-connected insiders, such as Halliburton and Blackwater.

We have seen an increase in abuses of executive privilege and secrecy, and of the nominating of partisan cronies and hacks. Among these were Harriet Miers, nominated to Justice of the Supreme Court and a prime example who did not get confirmed to the post, and two examples who did get confirmed: Mike Brown (ex-director for FEMA), who resigned after terrible consequences, and Attorney General Alberto Gonzales, who also had to resign after politicizing the whole of the Federal Attorney General Office.

We have seen an increase in the use of "signing statements"—whereby the president declares he does not intend to execute as written the law he is signing—to change the intent of laws passed by Congress—approximately 750 such statements according to the *Boston Globe* (Savage 2006), seemingly many more that all the previous presidents in aggregate. While the *Globe* does not specify how many signing statements were signed by President Reagan—when the practice started in earnest—it states that President Clinton signed approximately 140 in eight years, and that President George H. W. Bush signed 232 in four years.

A New Spin on an Old Yarn

These are a few reminders of what staying the course means. But along comes now the new image of Senator John McCain, the "Maverick and Champion of Change." To shore up his electability, over the last year Senator McCain has changed his stances on immigration, first amendment rights of lobbyists, and even the role of activist religion in government. He has been trying to spin out a new McCain, even using and politicizing his American hero story as he never did before to increase his "right-wing hawk" credentials and pandering to evangelical and Pentecostal leaders he once called "agents of intolerance" (Knowlton 2000).

To further convince the American electorate, Governor Palin was chosen to complete the new image. The Republican campaign is about remaking Senator McCain's image into a true agent of change that is promising to "shock the system" and bring new, maverick blood to Washington, while maintaining "Republican values." Palin is presented as a tough, eloquent, non-nonsense woman. She is the perfect accessory to complete McCain's makeover.

But what we have seen as the new image is spun out is the naked truth: Senator McCain is a diehard Republican who will do anything to get elected and will continue the policies of his predecessor, to the extent that Imperial Presidency will once again be an apt description. Governor Palin's selection process was pure party cronyism, superseding credentials and experience with loyalty and ideology. She is a Republican: her record on taxes is regressive, increasing sales taxes and decreasing property taxes, using budget surpluses for taxpayer bonuses while increasing the debt by borrowing for infrastructure projects; growing her government with inexperienced staff vowing loyalty to her, while going after her political enemies to the extent that they are afraid to talk about her in Alaska; and abusing earmarks to her political advantage and convenience in an unprecedented way. Her government largesse applies to herself even—who has ever heard of a mayor in a town of 9,000 collecting a salary of $64,000? Oh, that's right: she cut her salary down from $68,000—and hired a (loyal) city administrator to do her job, increasing the overall payroll (Yardley 2008).

Are they really agents of change? Are they the "mavericks" who will transform our government? Do they really represent the "new way" of doing things, the "new and improved" Republican way? As facts are revealed, the naked truth stands. Senator McCain's choice of Governor Palin reveals his commitment to staying the course—the Old Republican way. When, I wonder, will somebody point at him and shout out that the emperor has no clothes?

How to Lose an Election: A Fictional Glimpse into the Future

September 12, 2008

The following is a satirical take on the state of the election right after the Republican convention, which gave Senator McCain a boost. At that point, according to most polling data, Senator Obama lagged behind, for a week or so (see appendix A). For all of Senator Obama's supporters, it was worrisome to see the favorable spin on McCain and Palin that dominated the news at that time.

***

Four weeks after November 4 everybody is still trying to figure out what went wrong. Which were the key problems that made Senator Obama lose? What happened? Many possible explanations are circulating, among them the Sarah Palin effect, the overestimation of the youth vote, the effect of the swing states, and others. As I watch the news and read the newspapers, these are the main explanations that seem to be considered.

Underestimating the Sarah Palin Effect:

There were seemingly three possible approaches to Governor Palin's effect on the Republican ticket: depict her as a die-hard, old-fashioned, double-talking Republican, go further and expose her as an extreme religious activist that wants to merge church and state, or basically ignore her. Going for the attack just played into a great part of the Republican election strategy, which was to make Governor Palin a foil to deflect attention from Senator McCain. The more Governor Palin was attacked, the less attention people paid to Senator McCain while such attacks energized the Republican base more and more. Her likeability and the identification with the "non-elite" was a difficult angle to tackle. The question to ask should have been: *"OK, so I would like to go to a hockey game and drink a beer with her and the First Dude, but do I really want her making decisions on _____* (fill in the blank: social security, financial market regulations, access to health care, education, NATO and the National Security Council, the selection of Supreme Court Justices, or on whether the President is fit to discharge his duties)? Are we really sure we want another 'beer buddy' (albeit disguised as a 'hockey mom') in the White House?" Hiring a beer buddy, C student for the White House has cost us a lot already these last eight years. Maybe, the best way to counter the Sarah Palin effect would have been to mostly ignore her—except on the credibility issue—and never ever ridicule her from within the campaign (it is too easy and obviously expected by Republican strategists, banking on the "everyone's mom" image). The focus should have been on Senator McCain again and again and again.

Being Overconfident in the Message Getting Through:

Senator Obama kept saying *"when the dust settles, the American people will see the difference."* With the conventions, the debates, and the Sarah Palin effect, unfortunately there was so much dust in the air that it couldn't settle in time for the election. A big fan was required to clear out the dust, not simple gravity. The most powerful fan could have been President Bill Clinton. Senator Obama's campaign should have used anything in their power to get Bill Clinton on board and campaigning actively and decisively for Obama.

Believing in the Crowds:

It is easy to lose sight of the actual support within a region when facing large friendly crowds. With so little time left, it was tempting to give in to those big rallies. Big rallies are certainly a key base-energizing tool, a tool to send out surrogates to get out the vote. To reach the voters that were not energized, however, a greater TV exposure was required. Time was a constraint, but winning was also important! Senator Obama should have done more national TV interviews; at least three or four interviews a week on cable and broadcast—as he started in September with *World Week in Review, The O'Reilly Factor,* and *Countdown with Keith Olberman*. The reach to dissipate the "unknown" Obama factor should have been extended continuously and frequently.[7]

Overestimating the Youth Effect:

Getting out the youth vote turned out to be harder than what it seemed. Massive amounts of voting age youths were busy studying, working or more interested in MTV, partying or sleeping than in going to vote. In New Hampshire, during the primaries, given the crowds, the enthusiasm, and the polling numbers it seemed that Senator Obama would win over Senator Clinton. Unfortunately, because of those same polls, those young voters thought that someone else would go vote, so they did not have to. The message "every vote counts" did not get through, and Senator Obama lost the New Hampshire primary (39 percent Clinton vs. 37 percent Obama). At the general election, the same indolence led to lower numbers of young voters at the booths than was predicted by the polls.

Disregarding Key Swing States:

On August 26, 2008 around 3,500 ballots were "lost" in Palm Beach County, Florida. With a new voting system in place, the secretary of state required speedy certification of the results for the statewide elections. This was no problem for smaller counties but for the biggest ones, Palm Beach, Broward, and Miami-Dade (the most Democratic counties as well), this meant the possibility of not being able to count and recount on time, even for a small turnout such as the one that day. Was this a practice run for a general election voter manipulation?

Again in Florida shortly after this special election, on September 10, it was reported that a voter registration law (the "no match" law), that had been suspended on account of implementation problems, was reinstated by Secretary of State Kurt Browning. This law requires additional paperwork to document voter eligibility, and potentially requires registered voters to produce eligibility documentation on Election Day, when they go to vote. Of course, this made it harder for voter registration drives to work at crunch time, as well as turning off voters on Election Day that were given provisional ballots and instructions on how to make their vote count—within just two days.

In Florida, a three-pronged approach (in addition to checking on the results certification factor) may have worked: energizing the youth/change base by using Caroline Kennedy and Chelsea Clinton, and possibly Debbie Wasserman-Schultz, Ron Klein, or some other young congresspersons in rallies at FSU, FAU and FIU; using senators Clinton and Biden again, and again and again in Century Villages, Jewish temples, and Miami Beach, as well as the I-4 Corridor; using Senator Bill Nelson throughout the state, but primarily in the I-4 Corridor and the Northern East Coast. Of course, Senator Obama needed to be in Florida at least three times again. The intention should have been to win the state, not just to divert Republican resources, to make a significant difference in the Electoral College, and to protect that win! It was necessary to win in Florida and in Michigan (which also has a Republican secretary of state), and Indiana (again, also with a Republican secretary of state), and Ohio, and Pennsylvania. The Rust Belt was overrun by Governor Palin and her populist persona and rhetoric, and not enough was done about it. After all, in that region it was *only* her against Governor Ed Rendell, Senator Evan Bayh and Senator Joe Biden, as well as the Clintons (see *Palin Effect*, above).

Not Attacking:

The second day of the Republican convention was a barrage of attacks, personal and political on Senator Obama. Despite Senator McCain's assurances that he would run a "positive campaign" (see box 1) his campaign clearly backed off from that promise. A sense of righteous outrage against blatant lies, falsehoods, and misrepresentations was not transmitted by the Obama camp as a reaction to these. After all, everyone knew they were lies, didn't they? After all, the important part was how Senator Obama responded to these characterizations, right? But a clear picture of the of the Republican candidate's demagoguery, politicking, and his ideological continuity with the current administration was not portrayed with sufficient impact.

AKP&D Media[8] had its work cut out in this area. It had to work to earn its bucks by reviewing key counties in swing areas and crosschecking them against the survey polls for potential negatives in order to establish the impact message, the message that would swing the undecideds to choose Obama. On the issue front: Is it the economy? Is it health care? Is it home ownership? Is it security? On the attack front: Do Republicans stand for change? Can they improve your pocketbook? Can you trust lobbyists and flip-floppers?

For voters who do not tune in until after Labor Day, sound bites at the end of the campaign are the bases for their decision, so these sound bites should have been more incisive and direct. This is where campaign sloganeers and strategists earn their keep. Major campaign stops needed to be scheduled in swing sectors of swing counties of swing states to tout these slogans, and they were overlooked. Sound bite zingers needed to be spread in campaign messages and slogans, particularly in swing counties.

Going Wonk:

Senator Obama's spots and sound bites in September were long on exposition and short on zingers. For the final stretch, last minute vot-ers—those who say "I am not interested in politics" and make a superficial decision close to the end—the "wonk approach" does not work. The "wonk voters" are most likely already on the decided column, whether Democratic or Republican. Quick sound bites with clear and consistent contrast are required to get the message through to that undecided "last minute voter." Perhaps going a little negative, but highlighting the dif-ferences, a series of small ten-second spots exposing Senator McCain's

Box 1
Senator McCain Promises a Positive Campaign

At the beginning of their campaign, the McCain camp sent a copy of this memo from campaign manager Rick Davis to reporters, to announce their intention to conduct a positive, respectful, issue driven campaign

To: Campaign Leadership
From: Rick Davis
Subject: McCain Message
Date: 3/11/2008

John McCain is now the presumptive nominee of the Republican Party. It is critical, as we prepare to face off with whomever the Democrats select as their nominee, that we all follow John's lead and run a respectful campaign focused on the issues and values that are important to the American people.

Throughout the primary election we saw John McCain reject the type of politics that degrade our civics, and this will not change as he prepares to run head-to-head against the Democratic nominee.

John McCain will continue to run on his principles and will focus on the future of our country. The stakes could not be higher in this election, and John will contrast his vision for America with that of Senators Clinton and Obama. He will draw sharp contrasts: victory versus surrender to Islamic extremism; lower taxes and spending versus more big government; free-market solutions to health care versus costly mandates; and the appointment of strict constructionist judges versus those who legislate from the bench.

Overheated rhetoric and personal attacks on our opponents distract from the big differences between John McCain's vision for the future of our nation and the Democrats'. This campaign is about John McCain: his vision, leadership, experience, courage, service to his country and ability to lead as commander in chief from day one.

Throughout his life John McCain has held himself to the highest standards and he will continue to run a respectful campaign based on the issues. We expect that all supporters, surrogates and staff will hold themselves to similarly high standards when they are representing the campaign. To help guide you, please find talking points below.

This is an exciting time for our country and our Party. Thank you for your dedication and hard work. We face a great challenge this November: John is ready, and with your continued support I am confident we will succeed.

Thank you.

This memo was posted on realclearpolitics.com

tactics and showcasing Senator Obama's proposals could have gone something like this:

Spot 1: *Senator McCain would like you to believe that his tax proposals would benefit the middle class. According to independent studies the truth is that under Senator Obama's proposal the middle class would lower their taxes by 50 to 150 percent more. Yes, Senator Obama's plan proposes lower taxes for the middle class than Senator McCain's Proposal does. And the rich? Well they lower their taxes by more than 300 percent under McCain's ideas. Senator McCain distorts the truth to get elected. How can you trust Senator McCain to govern?*

Spot 2: *Senator McCain would like you to believe that teaching your children about "stranger danger" is wrong. When Senator Obama supported legislation to protect your children from sexual predators, Senator McCain called it "sex education for children." Senator McCain distorts the truth just to get elected. How can you trust Senator McCain to govern?*

Spot 3: *Senator McCain would like you to believe that he alone has a grasp of foreign policy and the war. He does not want timetables in Iraq, despite the fact that the Iraqi government wants one; and he wants us to get militarily involved in the Republic of Georgia because he has a lobbyist with interests there. Senator McCain supported a military dictator in Pakistan that was not doing enough to pursue Al-Qaeda. Senator McCain distorts the truth to get elected. How can you trust Senator McCain to govern?*

Spot 4: *Senator McCain would like you to believe that he will keep special interest lobbyists outside of his government. Yet his top campaign advisors are lobbyists for banking, oil, foreign governments, and other interests. Senator McCain distorts the truth to get elected. How can you trust Senator McCain to govern?*

Spot 5: *Senator McCain would like you to believe that he has a solution to America's health care crisis. His solution is to give more power to the insurance companies, and less to you. His solution includes gutting Medicare and Social Security. He doesn't care; he has a great health care plan for himself. By the way, that plan is the standard Senator Obama wants for every American. Senator McCain distorts the truth to get elected. How can you trust Senator McCain to govern?*

Spot 6: *Senator McCain would like you to believe that he identifies closely with religious leaders. He called Jerry Falwell and Pat Robertson "agents of intolerance." He looked to find a preacher to endorse him and found John Hagee, but dropped his endorsement soon after when it was no longer politically convenient. Senator McCain distorts the truth to get elected. How can you trust Senator McCain to govern?*

The trust issue as a factor regarding Senator McCain goes directly to his American Hero entitlement. The belief that we should trust him because of the honor he deservedly earned on account of his war service does not have a direct correlation with managing the country. He can be a war hero, but we still do not have to trust him to govern the nation.

***

As I click the *send* button on my computer, distributing these rambling thoughts to my email list of friends, family, and my Obama camp and "Newsie" crowd (Axelrod, Todd, et al.), I keep thinking that I cannot decide what it was that made Senator Obama lose the national election. Perhaps it was only one of these factors, maybe a combination of these factors, or of all of these factors. For an election that was for the Democrats to lose, we seem to have done a fine job at doing just that. Losing focus and being overconfident got us close to almost losing the primary. That was the dress rehearsal and, as they say, practice makes perfect. We got it right this time: we lost the presidential election.

Earmarks, Lobbyists, and Special Interests that Go Bump in the Night

September 24, 2008

The federal government centralizes decisions affecting innumerable people and multiple organizations throughout the nation. Seemingly detached and remote, decisions made in the corridors of the Capitol—or nearby—affect everyday life in any given community, big or small, in the U.S. But the government *is* detached and remote, far away, in Washington, DC. It is in the way that the government gathers information to make decisions affecting local communities and groups that sometimes politicking and misstatements are made for the sake of political populism.

A triad of mechanisms has developed for the gathering and flowing of information which the legislative and executive branches need in order to propose, establish, and implement policy. These mechanisms, because of the organic way in which they developed, with little structure or oversight, have been easily abused and can negatively impact the national budget. The appropriation of funds for special projects or the enacting of privileged treatment for particular groups can be necessary, many times fair, but can also be easily abused if there is no transparency; a blanket condemnation of earmarks, lobbyists, and special interest committees thus does not clearly address the problem that, as usual in politics, is not a clear-cut issue.

Representation by Earmark Proxy

The *Seattle Times* recently defined earmarks as "pet projects that members of Congress fund but that no federal agency has requested." (Bernton and Heath 2008). That is a concise description, albeit value laden. It is our elected officials' responsibility to look out for us, his or her constituents, as they are our representatives. The term "earmark" has now entered into the common political jargon as a fundamental flaw in the budget process: "pet projects" that no one else has requested. Senator Obama seemingly entered this discussion from a different angle, defining the problem as "earmark abuse," which is very different and addresses the actual definition of "earmark."[9]

The so-called earmarks are a fundamental part of our system of political representation. Our officials, when in tune with their constituencies, identify local projects that cannot be funded locally but represent an improvement to the community in either infrastructure or social services. Sometimes a community is so small or the need is so great that it requires assistance from the federal government to bring the expectation of the "American Way of Life" into the area. All of us are in the U.S., after all—and what is good for one community is good for the greater all. In the 2008 federal budget of $2.9 trillion, it is estimated that less than 1 percent is actually designated "earmarks" (Office of Management and Budget 2008).[10] However, that is still a considerable sum: $16.5 billion in fiscal 2008. The potential for wasteful spending is there, with more than $330 million earmarked funds on average for every state in the union.

The demagoguery surrounding the earmark issue should be tread upon carefully. Senator McCain has avowedly been opposed and been on record against earmarks for his state, Arizona. That is why, for example, a flood control project in Nogales, Arizona languished for years, and poor neighborhoods were subjected to severe damage every rainy season when the Army Corps of Engineers could not get funding for the drainage and canalization projects required. The state of repair and the network of roads in Arizona have been generally characterized as deplorable (Lilly 2008).

Alaska, on the other hand, is the largest state of the Union and arguably the most underdeveloped, so it makes sense to have a large proportion of

Figure 2
Analysis of the databases of Taxpayers for Common Sense by Center for
American Progress Action Fund Senior Fellow Scott Lilly. (Lilly 2008)

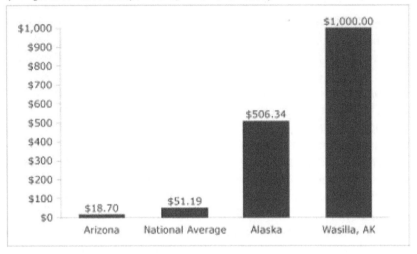

Per Capita Federal Earmark Funding
(All figures for 2008 except Wasilla, which is for 2002)

federal infrastructure projects in such a territory; more so than, say, in a small urbanized state such as Delaware (Office of Management and Budget 2008). When Governor Palin comes out generally against earmarks she must be careful about the way she portrays the issue; an issue that is not as clear cut as she and Senator McCain seem to be argue.[11]

Her contradictions in order to present herself as a champion against abuses in government spending have been revealed by the facts. The *Seattle Times* reported, for example that she said in the *News-Miner* (an Alaska local newspaper) that she had slashed the Alaska earmark requests by nearly two-thirds, down from $550 million in 2007 to just under $200 million. Except that the base figure for 2007 was $254 million, not $550 million, so her cuts this year were only 22 percent, not the 63 percent she claimed (Bernton et al. 2008). The accompanying graphic illustrates figures for earmarks in Alaska, Wasilla, the nation, and Arizona.

It is the elected representative's duty to seek out and identify the social and infrastructure needs that will improve the welfare of his or her community and to seek funds to satisfy these needs. It is when abuse, mismanagement and unauthorized diversion of requests and appropriated funds enter the picture that we must cry "foul." But the mayor, governor or congressman trying to look out for the interest of his or her constituents is part and parcel of what representative government is all about. And when populist demagogues make the eradication of earmarks an electoral issue, it should be clear that they are making promises that they not just can't keep but that they *shouldn't* keep.

Our Favorite Friend We Love to Hate: The Lobbyist

The next great scapegoat making rounds this political season is the lobbyist. Each side in the campaign tries to demonize the other by associating their opponent's staff with "Washington lobbyists" and lobbyist firms. The assertion and presumption is that influence peddling is rampant and Jack Abramoff wannabes are perverting the proper functioning and clear thinking of our elected officials.[12] But major corporations and interest groups—even towns in Alaska—are legitimate constituents to our federal government, and they too have a right to participate in policy formulation. When advocates are hired by businesses or specialty groups to argue their causes they are exercising this right.[13] Again, it is when abusing the system that this becomes a major obstacle to transparent government.

Overall, however, lobbying is a loosely structured mechanism, and its weaknesses have been seen in the past, most recently and notoriously with Jack Abramoff, of course. Regulating access and primarily ensuring full disclosure of lobbying and lobbying activities could help move this important aspect of government and policy formulation out from the shadows.

And, What about Those Special Interests?

What many lobbyists are to the left, many special interests are to the right. Again the "special interests" seem to be one of those Washingtonian ghouls that children near K Street should be afraid of at night. If you realize that groups labeled as "special interests" in the past have included the suffragettes, the NAACP, and the AFL-CIO you may get a different perspective on this moniker. For example, the unions supported child labor laws during the Great Depression because it was better for their members, in effect protecting and regulating the use of minors as labor force. Society is not worse off because of that.

It is within the context of governmental policy implementation that issue can, may and should be taken against the triad of special interests, lobbyists and earmarks. Our government needs information, needs to listen to its constituents, and needs collaboration from the affected parties in order to be responsive and representative; otherwise, we would be living in a centralized elected dictatorship. It is to the extent that abuses are committed, or skewed morals and corruption exist in the communicating, spinning, and filtering of the information needed for policy decisions, that these hobgoblins of politics are nefarious. Government is made up by men and women with all sorts of backgrounds, upbringings, character, and moral values. It is probable that there will always be abuses within this triad of representative mechanisms. It is the moral leadership and values from the top that will allow the flourishing of true representation and dialogue, and stamp out the abuses that these important mechanisms are naturally prone to.

Notes

1. In a widely panned speech, in front of a green background and obviously reading from a teleprompter, Senator McCain's contrasted poorly with the well-choreographed speech by Senator Obama and the poise of Senator Clinton. Senator Clinton did not recognize Senator Obama's nomination clinching feat that night and it was not only until a few days later that she suspended her campaign, in her "18 Million Cracks in the Ceiling" speech, effectively ending the primary process on June 5, 2008.
2. A few days before the Democratic National Convention in Denver, Senator Ted Kennedy became gravely ill, which could have suggested to Senator Clinton a path to follow in the Senate, as Senator Ted Kennedy's successor in the political universe, albeit still paying some political seniority dues.
3. Senator Clinton and President Clinton in fact supported Senator Obama's presidential campaign forcefully, especially in those regions where she had demonstrated strong resonance during the primaries.
4. This is a commonly quoted statement which comes from a letter to his wife, Abigail Adams on December 19, 1793. Among many places, it is cited in *The Yale Book of Quotations*, Fred R. Shapiro and Joseph Epstein, eds. (New Haven, CT: Yale University Press, 2006).
5. These positions and statements were repeatedly reported in all media or stated by her in interviews, the vice presidential debate, or in stump speeches.
6. This is not a certified fact, but it circulated widely. It may be an unfair characterization of Governor Palin. Similar to this allegation is the one regarding the Wasilla public library, in which she admittedly did not ban books, but only asked if it could be done, a disturbing question in and of itself (Fritze 2008, Yardley 2008).
7. Even after Senator Obama won the election, a significant percent of Senator McCain voters still believed Senator Obama "is or has been a Muslim." A survey reported by Beliefnet found that almost 50 percent of McCain voters thought that was the case. According to the survey, conducted by Waldman and Gildoff (2008), "half of John McCain voters believe Barack Obama is or was a Muslim, while many more Obama voters say McCain ran an 'unchristian' campaign, rather than vice versa." The survey was advertised throughout Beliefnet's website and newsletters. From November 3 through November 6, 4,400 users completed the survey. Even though the methodology is not strict—Beliefnet states that "the survey is not scientific or based on random sampling"—such a result would suggest a degree of success in the disinformation campaign on this subject carried out by the Republican strategists.

8.   AKP&D Media, (Axelrod, Kupper, Plouffe and Del Cecato), was the advertising and communications consulting firm headed by David Axelrod and in charge of Senator Obama's campaign.

9.   President Bush signed Executive Order 13457 on January 29, 2008 that defines earmarks as "any funds provided by Congress for projects, programs, or grants where the congressional direction (whether in statutory text, report language, or other communication) (1) circumvents merit-based or competitive allocation processes; (2) specifies the location or recipient of the funds; or (3) otherwise limits the ability of the Executive Branch to manage its statutory and constitutional responsibilities for the allocation of federal funds" (Office of Management and Budget 2008).

10. FY 2008 lists $16,501,833,000 in appropriation or authorizations for earmark spending as defined in EO 13457, out of a total of $2,918 billion in outlays. This represents 0.57 percent of the federal budget allocated for earmarks in 2008, and $330 million average per State. In FY 2005, the numbers were $18.94 billion, $2,422 billion, 0.78 percent, and $379 million average per State. The OMB reports that figures for 2008 and 2005 may not be directly comparable, as earmarks were not clearly listed and defined in 2005 in the same manner as they are now (Office of Management and Budget 2008).

11. In terms of change and reduction, as comparable as the OMB has been able to make the different categories, earmarks under the Department of Transportation, for example, for 2008 were 50 percent of the amount allocated in 2005. By comparison, earmarks allocated under the Department of Homeland Security for 2008 were 1,926 percent of the funds allocated in 2005 (they grew from $27.9 million to $537.5 million). While not all allocation determinations have been assigned yet per state for FY 2008 Alaska has to date $154.9 million (approximately $226 per person) in appropriations, Arizona had $65.6 million ($11 per person), and Delaware had $37.3 million ($43 per person) (Office of Management and Budget).

12. Jack Abramoff is a convicted felon who worked as a lobbyist and who at his peak was a registered agent for fifty-one clients. At least eleven congressmen, former White House staffers and other lobbyists associated to Mr. Abramoff have been convicted of criminal charges related to bribery and influence peddling. The congressional investigations leading to Mr. Abramoff's eventual conviction were spearheaded by Senator John McCain.

13. Foreign countries and corporations are a special matter and there are laws that require additional regulation for agents representing foreign entities and governments. In a recent case in Miami, several Venezuelans were convicted for acting illegally primarily by failing to register as foreign agents in the U.S. for their participation in cash contributions by the Venezuelan government to the campaign of current Argentina President Cristina Fernández de Kirchner.

7

State of the Nation

As the national election unfolded, I addressed critical points of discussion related to our present condition and in response to particular events. These constituted mainly letters to editors of the *New York Times*, *Miami Herald* (and to Scott Andron, business editor, *Miami Herald*), *Washington Post*, and to my congressmen. Some of these essays were in progress as the news of the day unfolded and prompted a new response in the form of quick letters, which is why the dates seem so close to each other. Of course, some of these letters were either edited or were portions of the essays, which include the ones that follow.

A $700,000,000,000 Check

September 27. 2008

To the extent that irresponsible financial engineering devised incredibly complicated instruments that muddled the real value of America's assets, I support a plan that blows away the smoke and mirrors that the Wizards of Wall Street have used to sell everything but the Brooklyn Bridge to speculators who hoped they could resell it—or short sell it—at a profit. I do not support the idea that the same people who practiced such sleight of hand be the ones who manage the rescue and get their 1 percent ($7,000,000,000 of the $700,000,000,000–when you put in the zeros it looks bigger, doesn't it!) or whatever percentage for their efforts.

The financial markets have been used for rampant speculative profiteering; the proposed blank check is unfair to the American taxpayer who has been hoodwinked by these snake oil salesmen with MBAs. It is not fair that we should be forced to mortgage even more of our future to make sure that the darling boys of Wall Street can have their filet of flounder with fine Chardonnay and a clean conscience. The markets will go lower, yes; and brokerage firms will no longer exist as they once had, yes. But maybe it is time we went back to thinking that bankers should be a conservative, staid, and risk-averse bunch, just like Mr. George Banks, of *Mary Poppins* fame. What a concept: growth based on real assets as opposed to speculative assets! What we have seen over the last ten to fifteen years is an increase in the myth of "portfolio risk management," asset securitization, and creative financial leverage that has led us to a situation where, in fact, we were the proud owners of the Brooklyn Bridge or, even worse, of the "Bridge to Nowhere."

It is clear that we cannot let our financial system collapse and emergency measures are required to restore credit liquidity. It should also be clear that the solution is not more of the same.

A Few Days Later: The Financial "Bailout"

September 30, 2008

With a small window of reflection on the Bush/Paulson financial sector "bailout" proposal, clearly a bit of skepticism was warranted. Where did the quantification of that enormous sum come from? No true credible information has been presented to determine the amount of illiquid securitized instruments clogging the credit pipeline. Why is there an expectation that if the government buys the distressed assets of speculating financial institutions, these will eventually be sound and could be sold back at a profit? While the value of these securitized assets has generated great discussion—and an evaluation of accounting standards for debt valuation, mark-to-market, and fair value—the underlying value of these financially engineered securities seems to be—or so we are told—unsecured and bad mortgages for overvalued real estate, and mostly—or so we are told—homes. We are also told that, as opposed to the Resolution Trust Corporation created to manage the Savings & Loan rescue, there will be no overarching mechanism or independent institution to liquidate the real estate at the core of the crisis. The Treasury is expected to just hold the distressed financial instruments and sell them back to the market at a later time. If the underlying assets described remain at the core of the instruments however, then the likelihood of an increase in their value is not high—because they were overvalued to begin with! In a final resolution, to the extent that mortgages of primary residences are part of the distressed assets, these homes and their residents should be protected, and that would be a positive use of the spending authority under the "bailout" plan. This means the "unsecuritization" or unbundling of the financial instruments that created the credit crunch, which could then not be resold back to the market—as we have been demagogically told at a possible profit—because, obviously, they would no longer exist. This would probably represent a loss financially to the U.S. Treasury because the underlying asset—the real estate—lost value. But it would be a gain in social stability and security, reverting into a better economy. It would be a better use of the taxpayers' money than holding worthless paper with the false expectation that it will someday increase in value.

Outsider Influences: Monroe is Long Gone

September 30, 2008

Towards the end of the last century, Russia dismantled its main land-based intelligence gathering facility in the Western Hemisphere in Lourdes, Cuba. Russia has maintained some limited capabilities in the area using aerial intelligence gathering out of bases in San Antonio de Los Baños and Jose Martí, but the closing of Lourdes was seen by the hawks in Moscow as a major blow, both actually and morally, to the pride and capabilities of the Russian intelligence and its military apparatus. A blow brought upon them by the economic failure of the Motherland. The decrease in the Mighty Bear's power has been a thorn in its side and a source of wounded pride for its politicians ever since the fall of 1989, when the Berlin Wall was torn down. The Soviet Red Army, one of the largest standing armies in the world at the time, was shown to be ill equipped and trained, and soon was also reduced to a large extent, with the low point believed to have been in 1998—around the same time as the closing of Lourdes.

Now, it is estimated that over the last six years (2002-2008), Russia has quadrupled its military expenditures, now, once again, second only to the U.S. in this category. Former President and current Prime Minister Vladimir Putin has increasingly stirred nationalistic passion and pride within Russia and, given his actions, expects to bring his country back to superpower level.

Putin's ambition becomes more troubling when compounded with China's desire to extend its own influence in order to increase access to the basic commodities—oil, tin, copper, etc.—it requires to feed its gigantic economic growth, which in turn is being financed with the enormous trade surplus it has, especially with the United States. Our neglected neighbors to the South seem to be increasingly involved in this power flexing, and are doing some lifting of their own in this geopolitical chess playing.

Hugo Chávez

Within this context, along comes Colonel Hugo Chávez to court both sides, Russia and China. Colonel Chávez is a very effective, charismatic and personally charming politician who knows how to play the populist game in Venezuela and Latin America, feeding the egos of nationalists and playing wedge politics with a vengeance. He personifies the ideal of "the noble revolutionary" concept, first with his failed attempt at overthrowing the constitutional order by bloody force in the spring of 1992 and his follow-up that fall—with hundreds dead and many still missing—and then with his populist-based campaign, his election, and the subsequent successive changes to the constitution in order to progressively concentrate all state and economic power unto himself. His ambition to unify most of South America into an "anti-imperialist" bloc—the "empire" defined always as the U.S.—has him bringing in outside players in a way that makes the Monroe Doctrine patently obsolete.

It is believed that Colonel Chávez has been aligned to the communist ideology of Fidel Castro at least since the time he is rumored to have been assigned—actually requested to be assigned—to Castro's security detail on the occasion of the United Nations Conference of the Law of the Sea Session in Caracas in 1974.[1] Chávez graduated from the Military Academy as a lieutenant colonel in 1975, and founded MBR-200 in 1982. MBR-200 was an underground military subversive organization dedicated to the advancement of socialist ideals and inspired by Simon Bolivar's ideas, as interpreted by Chávez and the other group members. As Castro's ideological disciple, Chávez views the economic power of the U.S. as a threat to his ideal world view of the balance of power, which he qualifies as currently mono-polar—concentrated in one sole economic pole, namely the U.S. His actions point to plans for diluting and reducing his perceived power of the U.S. by increasing the influence of Russia and China in Latin America.

The Venezuelan economic dependence on the U.S. is structurally based on the oil refineries that are primarily engineered to process Venezuelan crude—a great majority of which are located in the U.S. Colonel Chávez is attempting to change that dependence by building refineries across the Caribbean and, as recently announced, in China. His increased commercial ties with China and his brokering of Chinese trade within Latin America is, in a way, not as disturbing as his increased arms purchases from and potential military alliances with Russia. Just as Chávez seeks to increase China's economic penetration into Latin America, he seems to want to increase Russian military presence in the region. In his most recent trip to Cuba, China and Russia, Chávez announced a $2 billion arms procurement deal from Russia, over the $3.4 billion procured between 2005-2006 (Reuters 2008b, Novosti 2008), hailing this nation as a "strategic partner," just as a contingent of Russia's Northern Fleet, including its flagship guided missile cruiser *Peter the Great* is heading towards the Caribbean for joint naval exercises with the Venezuelan navy. The Northern Fleet of the Russian navy includes also numerous submarines equipped with ballistic missiles.

These war games and military exercises are a way of both Russia and Venezuela needling the U.S. Especially Russia because of the insistence of the Bush U.S. administration in hawkishly and defiantly establishing military alliances with that country's border nations, Georgia and Ukraine particularly, as well as threatening to install ballistic weapons in Poland and radar in the Czech Republic. It is not out of the question at this time to believe that Venezuela may allow Russia to establish military outposts or bases in its Caribbean territories, including, for example a refueling station or similar token presence in Isla de Aves (just a few hundred miles from Puerto Rico), as part of an expanded Russian military infrastructure. After all, this years' Russian military budget is a historical record of approximately $40 billion (the United States' will be approximately $90 billion), and it is expected to rise to approx $58 billion by 2011 (Associated Press 2008).[2] Russia will be putting that new hardware somewhere.

As Chávez takes steps to sever economic ties with the U.S. through greater ties with Russia, China, and his Latin America partners, the U.S. must, as a security imperative, wean itself from the symbiotic dependency with Venezuela's (and for that matter all) oil. It is unquestionable that a sound energy policy becomes a strategic fundamental in terms of the safety and well being of the United States in an increasingly complex world.

Mercenary Terrorism

September 30, 2008

The most disturbing part of the seemingly neglected focus from the U.S. on our southern neighbors is complacency about the possible terrorist alliances between Islamic terrorists and the FARC (Fuerzas Armadas Revolucionarias de Colombia). The information is not totally clear but there seems to be a disturbing coincidence of numbers related to the alleged donation of $300 million that Colonel Chávez pledged to give to the FARC, the attempts by the FARC organization to purchase uranium, and the supposed value of the ($150 million, with "much more available")—as it turned out depleted—uranium ore (Washington Times 2008). This attempt to negotiate and traffic in the scariest of terror weapons is extremely disturbing. Given the approaches that Chávez has made towards the government of Iran; the establishment of routine flights between Teheran and Caracas and subsequent trade in heavy equipment export/import; the nefarious terrorist activities originated in Iran through Hezbollah in Latin America (remember AMIA, Buenos Aires);[3] the increasingly mercenary disposition of the cash starved FARC; and the smuggling capabilities of the FARC sponsored drug cartels, a series of events could be in place to release a purportedly radioactive, certainly toxic, and surely socially disruptive dirty weapon within the U.S. The amount of drugs seized (4,249 kilograms of cocaine just in the second quarter of 2007, according to the DEA) as compared to the still large amounts of cocaine consumed in the U.S. indicates a large smuggling capability by these terrorists. It is plausible to imagine an attempt to smuggle several packets of ten to fifteen kilograms each of depleted uranium to release them dramatically in some urban area or areas and create a grave panic and disruption, though probably not a major loss of life. While the posturing of Hugo Chávez is increasingly reckless and destabilizing, his association with the FARC and drug cartel mercenaries behind this potential plot brands him definitely as a sponsor of terrorism.

Notes

1. Though I have been unable to locate certifiable records for this fact, news accounts and personal observation make me believe this is true. At the time, in 1974, I was working in the same buildings (Parque Central, Caracas) where the Conference was held.
2. For more on military budgets around the world, visit GlobalSecurity.org. Specifically for Russia: http://www.globalsecurity.org/military/world/russia/mo-budget.htm.
3. The headquarters building of AMIA (Asociación Mutual Israelita Argentina) in Buenos Aires was bombed on July 18, 1994, killing eighty-five people and injuring hundreds. Interpol and the government of Argentina have determined that the bombing was planned by members of the government of Iran (the Red Army) and was executed by Hezbollah.

8

The Debates

The Debate Performances

October 7 to October 21, 2008

Ol' Miss (Oxford, Mississippi)

The first presidential debate, held in the Campus of the University of Mississippi, Oxford on September 26 did not effectively differentiate major breakthrough points between the candidates. Debates in general are last minute pitches in prime time to persuade undecided voters. These voters are looking for (a) a reason to vote for one of the candidates, or (b) a reason to vote against the other. At the time I write this (October 6), the Rasmussen polling service reports that 44 percent of voters say they will vote for Senator Obama and will not change their mind about it between now and Election Day, 38 percent say the same for Senator McCain, and 14 percent say they have a preference but might change their mind. The overall poll gives Senator Obama a 52 percent lead over McCain's 44 percent.

What the first debate did for some undecided and independents with both, the theatrics leading to it by Senator McCain, and by the demeanor of both candidates on stage, was to establish the presidential credibility of Senator Obama. There were many potential voters who had not seen Senator Obama under the light and with the contrast presented that night in Ol' Miss. Senator McCain's behavior the week preceding the debate—reacting and counter-reacting to the financial market's melt-down—seemed closer to that of a loose cannon than to that of a maverick (Halloran 2008).

The first point of interest and contrast through this debate was illustrated by the approaches to the current financial crisis. While substantive issues that could not truly be answered in a sound bite to the question *"what promises would you not keep?"*—paraphrasing the moderator, Jim Lehrer— Senator Obama seemed more reflexive about the issue of the day: the economy. Senator McCain's answer: "freeze spending" would in fact plunge the economy into a greater tailspin. This is a main street uninformed answer and a simplistic solution to a complex problem. At home, if you are in financial problems, you curtail spending because the money you spend leaves the house. When the government spends money it goes into the general economy, it does not disappear. Franklin Delano Roosevelt's answer to the Great Depression was not to cut spending but to increase it, with the Works Progress Administration and other programs. It is what makes sense. When Senator McCain says he is not very versed in economics, he really is talking straight. This is not to say that a WPA equivalent is required now, but to "freeze spending" would be a disaster.

The second point that night in Mississippi was something of great interest to me because it demonstrated a clear continuity of thought from Senator Obama. After the debate, many pundits gave a negative spin to how he said something along the lines of "Senator McCain is right…" several times—even his opponent used these lines in media ads later on. But this is part of negotiation techniques developed at Harvard—and popularized by William Ury, Roger Fisher, and James K. Sebenius, among others from *The Harvard Negotiation Project*, at Harvard Law School—that has been very successful in many settings. It is based on separating the people conducting the negotiation from the problems and issues at hand, and seeks to obtain win-win solutions. It seems that Senator McCain is unable to separate people from issues, as he was coached reflecting his character. It was obvious that he was instructed not to look directly at Senator Obama in order not to get overly rattled. He did not want to personalize him. He keeps calling him "my opponent." Given Senator McCain's training and the way he approaches the word "win," win-win does not seem to be within his conceptual framework.

When it comes to the small portion of the electorate that still has not decided or may still change their mind, in the first debate Senator Obama was a clear winner. This fact was clearly reflected in the subsequent intention to vote polls. Senator McCain missed this one at Ol' Miss. The strategy at this point for Senator Obama should be to maintain his leader-like demeanor and to allow his associates to continue highlighting the erratic behavior of Senator McCain—behavior that, as is coming to light now, has been a constant throughout his personal and professional life.

Washington University (St. Louis, MO)—The VP Contenders

In a show that was all about expectations and waiting for a train wreck from either side, the VP debate at first blush seemed to do nothing to change the endgame strategies of the campaigns. It was a reassuring presentation for both Senator McCain and Governor Palin's supporters, and for senators Obama and Biden's.

Governor Palin did not debate. She answered her own questions with non sequiturs and contradictions. She came across to the non-hypnotized, as the Stepford Candidate, robotically answering prefabricated answers that had nothing or little to do with Gwen Iffil's (the moderator's) questions, nor following up to Senator Biden's answers. Her self-absorption and ambition came across clearly as she coldly answered the question regarding succeeding the president if the need arose. She did wink and nod her way to the final bell, and left confident in her own self, ready now to take on the world by storm once again.

The *Wall Street Journal* columnist Peggy Noonan called Governor Palin's performance "an infomercial pitch for charm in politics" (Noonan 2008), but Governor Palin reminded me more of Mack the Knife, cozily cuddling up with a smile as he plunges into the side of his victim a fatal blow, then calmly walking away. Obviously trying to break out of the McCain constraints, she now has restarted with a vengeance the misinformation strategy regarding Senator Obama that was prevalent at the start of the election year. The true aftermath of this debate—where no one stumbled or gaffed—is that Sarah Palin is now loose and on the prowl, lipstick off and gloves on.

As the next debates come around, the personalization of issues will take a greater role in the McCain/Palin camp, and the strategy from the Democratic side might be to find reasons why a conservative voter should not vote for Senator McCain who is, after all, the top of the ticket. As a strategy, the Obama campaign should try to get people turned off by the McCain/Palin ticket, particularly in southern states such as Georgia, South Carolina, and Florida. Give them the naked truth about McCain: The loose cannon that wrecked and walked away from three Navy planes, including one alleged wreck in a private flight (Vartabedian and Serrano 2008)—plus the one he was shot down in, and not counting the accident on the *USS Forrestal*.[1] Is that the pilot that you want on board when the plane (our nation) is in distress? McCain, the senator who was associated with the S&L scandal, and pandered to evangelists and Pentecostals after calling them agents of intolerance, may not be the person you want in the White House come January 2009. These core character allegations may turn some conservative voters away from the voting booth on November 4.

The Belmont Stakes (Nashville, Tennessee)

The second presidential debate, on October 2, was high-risk stakes for Senator McCain. With the economic crisis looming, Senator Obama was gaining ground, no longer in a statistical tie, and playing offense in red states.

The debate, which played out as a town hall meeting, lacked high drama or major gaffes once again. After all, that is the way the candidates were seeking to perform. Senator McCain tried to trump the night with a surprise economic program to rescue homeowners in economic distress, but he neither played it out throughout the debate nor thought it out before hand. His claim *"it is my program, not President Bush's, not Senator Obama's"* was bold, but will probably bring negative consequences to his campaign, both from his own conservative base and from the financial sector. Besides that one, Senator McCain did not have any other major highlights during that debate. Senator Obama came across as more forceful, even when talking about terrorism: *"We will kill Bin Laden; we will crush Al Qaeda,"* as opposed to Senator McCain's *"I am not going to telegraph my punches (to the enemy)"* which, in contrast, seemed lame.

In a previous essay I had suggested that the series of Town Hall debates that Senator McCain had proposed could be favorable to Senator Obama. These strategies are difficult to gauge: even though there is no question that Senator Obama had better demeanor, better presence and better arguments in the Belmont University town hall debate, it could be that it was in this single instance on national TV that Senator Obama outshone Senator McCain in a town hall. Maybe in a series of ten the effect would balance, and that could be an advantage loss for Senator Obama. With this one instance and with the benefit of scarcity, or by overcoming the contempt of familiarity and the clutter of frequency, Senator Obama in fact proved to have an altogether better debate strategy. Yes, it is true that he probably would have shone in more town hall debates than his opponent. But this way, with only one, it was a clear show stopper. In the Belmont Stakes, Senator Obama made a clear bid for the Triple Crown.

Last Showdown in Hofstra (Hampstead, New York)

The third presidential debate, held October 15, had an interesting format, with moderator Bob Schieffer turning his back to the audience, sitting at a table with both candidates, who were angled towards each other and to the theater audience at the same time. To us, the TV watchers, what we got was a close up split screen of each candidate, simultaneously comparing one candidate's reaction to the other's statements (at least on C-SPAN, where I watched). This was not favorable to Senator McCain, who came across as angry and fidgety, occasionally eyeing "that one" (which, we later learned, translates as "Barack" in Swahili[2]).

Again the debate was carefully controlled by Senator Obama who avoided the baiting that Senator McCain continuously used in order to try to elicit an angry response. Perhaps Senator Obama was in fact a little too composed when answering the unfounded questions and addressing the double talk by Senator McCain. With no major pratfalls or gaffes here by either one, the debate could be said did bring out Senator McCain's best performance, as he tried to raise issues and doubts about Obama that, anyway, have been answered already again and again. However, Senator McCain's performance was not better than Senator Obama's.

The most interesting or, in a skewed way, entertaining issue of the debate was the thrusting into the spotlight of "Joe the Plumber," mentioned according to some media counts around twenty-six times, more than any other issue, such as Iraq, education, or abortion. The use by Senator McCain of Mr. Samuel Joseph Wurzelbacher was an attempt to sandbag Senator Obama on the taxes issue, using a statement by a person that enjoyed his moment in the spotlight by posing a question but not listening to an answer. It is unfortunate that this seems to be the type of "policy advisors" that Senator McCain does listen to. It would seem better for the country—if the priority is "country first"—to listen to real experts in economic and fiscal policy such as Robert Solow, Joseph Stieglitz, Warren Buffet, George Soros, Paul Volcker, and Arthur Levitt—all of whom, by the way, support Senator Obama. Joe the Plumber is a voice that needs to be heard, all right, as he represents a portion of America; but his is not the voice of expertise to be used when defining policy. Furthermore, Joe seems misinformed about the two alternatives since, in his case, it actually seems that he would personally benefit more under Senator Obama's economic, social and health plans than under Senator McCain's proposals (see below: *The Plumber's Taxes*).

However, for Senator McCain it was not the issue that counted. He used Joe's voice not to address substantive tax policy or to focus on real differences; he used it to pull off a populist stunt. We should all be *tired* of populist stunts, shouldn't we? Just because of his use of Joe the Plumber in this manner, Senator McCain gets a failing grade in the debate at Hofstra University.

Finally, there is one more point that needs to be made. Within the volleys of topics and plumber distractions of this debate, some important moments almost went by unnoticed. I thank Douglas W. Kmiec for reminding me of a particular moment.[3] In an insightful article published on the op-ed page of the *Miami Herald*, Kmiec writes (Kmiec 2008):

> In the final presidential debate Wednesday, Obama had seemingly finished giving his view on abortion when he added these words: Abortion is "always a tragic situation," he said, and we should "try to prevent unintended pregnancies by providing appropriate education to our youth, communicating that sexuality is sacred...and providing options for adoption and helping single mothers if they want to choose to keep the baby.... Nobody is pro-abortion.... We should try to reduce these circumstances."

The platform adopted at the Democratic National Convention included a defense of the legalization of abortion but with the qualifier that it should be rare—a statement originally used during President Clinton's administration. It went on to outline the series of policies and initiatives directed to making this painful issue a rare circumstance, engaging in effective sex education and supporting options for mothers who choose to have their baby. This, as Kmiec pointed out and as Senator Obama tried to get across during this final debate, is a more effective approach to reducing unwanted pregnancies than the high schoolish "promise rings" and abstinence policies favored by the likes of Governor Palin, and demonstrably ineffective when it comes to preventing something as basic as teenage pregnancies.

A Homeowner's Bailout

October 8, 2008

Senator McCain's homeowner bailout program proposed during the Belmont University debate is directed to the reinforcement of one of the fundamentals of the economy: home ownership. The idea is sound, and is already possible using the authority conferred to the Treasury under the Troubled Asset Relief Program (TARP). Under the umbrella of the TARP, unbundling the securities backed by upside down mortgages might clear up some of the grime clogging up our economy's wheels.

But, although it is sound to propose a program to assist troubled homeowners, I cannot help but think that this proposal comes out of somewhat partisan political desperation, just for electoral gain. I have to think that because of the seemingly contradictory and incomplete ideas developed by Senator McCain during the debate.

Senator McCain said during the debate that he called out Fannie Mae and Freddie Mac when these institutions were backing mortgages for people who could not really afford homes. It is odd, however, that right after slamming the promotion of home ownership—the mission of the Federal National Mortgage Association and the Federal Home Mortgage Corporation—Senator McCain then turns around and suggests a program that will duplicate the TARP and Fannie Mae/Freddie Mac's roles, disregarding that duplicate programs promote inefficiencies and dilute responsibilities, not to mention increase bureaucracy. This seems to be a throwback to his experience with the Resolution Trust Corporation (RTC), suggesting an institution similar to that one which helped resolve the Savings & Loan debacle. While the RTC worked for the S&L crisis, in this instance a different set of problems exist because the insolvency of the banks' balance sheets comes from financial instruments with an imponderable market value, not real assets, so the TARP should be intrinsically part of any such program.

The way Senator McCain promoted his plan as an independent program in the October 2 debate was a populist way of promoting the idea of protecting the homeowners most affected by the real estate crunch on the economy. What needs to be done is to find the securities that bundled these homeowners' mortgages and offer the relief that the TARP has already authorized the Treasury to enact for these homeowners.

The Plumber's Taxes

October 16, 2008

In a disappointing response to the "Joe the Plumber" sandbag, Senator Obama failed to make two points clear: If Mr. Joe Wurzelbacher is fortunate enough to be actually taking home more than $250,000 a year, then he is among the top 5 percent of income earners in the U.S. and yes, his taxes may go up slightly under Obama's plan—back to Clinton's levels according to Senator Obama, although some analysts suggest that they will not even raise to that level. According to the charts prepared by the *Washington Post* and redrawn by Viveka Wiley, based on Tax Policy Center analyses (Burman et al. 2008), it seems that Joe may not even experience a tax increase—but he probably would under his own regressive idea of a flat tax. (See figure 3.)

In addition to that, the second point that Senator Obama failed to address clearly was that, even if Joe's personal taxes on his take home pay were to increase, him and countless other service providers in the U.S. will benefit from the additional disposable income provided to the 85 to

Figure 3

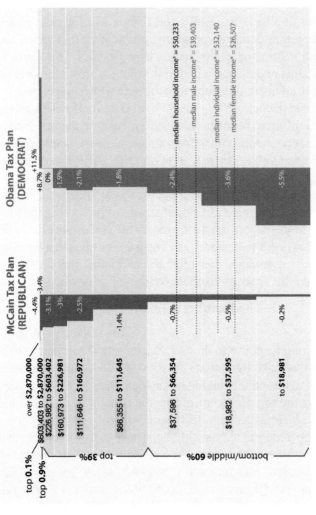

Source: Tax Plan data from Washington Post reporting of Tax Policy Center analysis. Redrawn to scale with height of bars corresponding to population of each group, as given in original TPC data.

US Presidential Candidates tax plans, redrawn from Washington Post data by Viveka Weiley - http://chartjunk.karmanaut.com

95 percent of the rest of the working Americans receiving an effective tax cut. Senator Obama failed to stress the point that his promised job creation programs as well as the business tax credits directed to bringing back manufacturing jobs to America will improve the American economy and will generate a positive cycle of cash flow and investments that will reenergize the economy. These programs, in addition to possibly stimulating hiring in Joe's own company, will give other Americans the possibility of having the income necessary to hire his services. Jobs are not handouts given by business owners; they are resources that business owners use in order to increase sales and profits. If the economy is good, it makes sense to hire in order to capitalize on available disposable incomes in the most effective way. The plans laid out by Senator Obama's economic team are in fact positive for Mr. Wurzelbacher's future business and income. I hope the senator is clear enough on his own plan to counter argue when confronted with misinformed and distorting comments such as those of "Joe the Plumber."

Though at the macroeconomic level Senator Obama's plan is unquestionably better for Mr. W's business and income in the short and long runs, it would be an interesting accounting exercise to review the actual business plan and/or profit/loss statements of Mr. W's business in order to compare results under both economic proposals, Senator Obama's and Senator McCain's.

Endorsements

October 19, 2008

This has been a week of endorsements. The newspapers that I regularly read: the *Los Angeles Times*, the *Washington Post*, the *Miami Herald*, and the *New York Times* editorial board all endorsed Senator Obama. A cursory search finds a string of other newspaper endorsements for Senator Obama: the *Chicago Tribune* (as expected for a native son), the *Philadelphia Inquirer* (with a strange, dissenting opinion that ineffectively describes a Senator McCain that has not been around the campaign for a long time now), the *San Francisco Chronicle*, the *Seattle Post Intelligencer* and other newspapers from "blue" states that perhaps reflect that "elite media" Governor Palin talks so much about.[4]

But there are interesting endorsements, from other (non elite?) newspapers that raise an eyebrow: the *Denver Post*, the *Salt Lake Tribune*, the *New York Daily News* (ok, not really in a red state), the *Houston Chronicle*, the *Austin American Statesman*, the *Las Vegas Sun* and others. All of these endorsed George W Bush in 2004 as did the *Chicago*

Tribune and the *Long Beach Press Telegram*, in Los Angeles. All in all, Senator Obama has accumulated the endorsement of ninety-five newspapers around the country as of this date–according to a current tally in Wikipedia– of which at least twenty-two (23 percent) endorsed GWB in 2004, whereas Senator McCain has twenty-six endorsements, including the *New York Post* (no surprise here), the *Washington Examiner* (ditto), the *Tampa Tribune*, and the *Amarillo Globe News* among others. Of his endorsements to date, only one, the *Daily Press* in Newport News, Virginia, endorsed John Kerry in 2004. This paper has a caveat on Governor Palin in their endorsement, saying they would have preferred Governor Romney on the ticket. For a perspective on proportion, John Kerry had received 213 endorsements by Election Day 2004 and George W. Bush had received 205—51 percent Kerry vs. 49 percent Bush. At this moment the tally stands at 79 percent Obama vs. 21 percent McCain in newspaper endorsements around the nation.

While the list of newspaper endorsements is impressive, other positions by "elite media" members shed additional light into Senator Obama's appeal. These include lukewarm repudiations of Senator McCain behavior and decisions by conservative thinkers such as George Will and Kathleen Parker, as well as outright endorsements from the likes of Wick Allison and Christopher Buckley. We are still waiting to see what Peggy Noonan has to say.[5] A common thread among repudiations and endorsements has been a criticism of the selection of Governor Palin as running mate and the wedge politics being played out by the Republican campaign.

The most stunning endorsement came today with General Colin Powell's backing of Senator Obama. The significance of this endorsement cannot be diminished by early reactions such as those by George Will and Rush Limbaugh suggesting that it was a matter of racial politics. Senator McCain's initial reaction was surprising also, given that the endorsement had been rumored hours in advance. Senator McCain's counterargument was that he had the endorsement of four former secretaries of state and many generals and admirals. He seems to miss the point: General Colin Powel was a Republican secretary of state, just like the four who endorse Senator McCain; and he was Bush 43's to boot! It was to be expected that a dismissal of the importance of this endorsement by McCain's camp would be forthcoming. But McCain's and Palin's obviously coached answer was very weak, especially given the arguments that General Powell set forth on *Meet the Press* in favor of Senator Obama and against Senator McCain. General Powell's arguments were about leadership during crises and judgment in government, both tests ("Final Exam" were his words) which he said Senator McCain has failed and Senator Obama has passed over the last few weeks since the conventions. He added that the use of wedge and divisive politics is counterproductive to the country in this time of economic and military crises. His key words, regarding Senator Obama, were: "he has met the standard of being a successful president, being an exceptional president. I think he is a transformational figure. He is a new generation coming into the world—onto the world stage, onto the American stage, and for that reason I'll be voting for Senator Barack Obama."

Senator McCain's response to that strong endorsement by a former member of President Bush's Cabinet—a national security advisor and chairman of the Joint Chiefs of Staff during the first Gulf War under Bush 41—was not effective. Once again, the lack of preparation and the disarray was evident in Senator McCain's campaign. This endorsement is a reaffirmation of the transformational nature of Senator Obama as "Obama Republicans" trump "Reagan Democrats" in this moment of our history.

Notes

1.   On July 29, 1967, the worst fire on a U.S. Navy ship since World War II broke out on the *USS Forrestal* in the Gulf of Tonkin, near Vietnam. A missile accidentally fired off an F-4 Phantom II airplane, striking other planes, including one next to the plane Lt. Commander John McCain had just climbed into. Casualties were 134 sailors killed, 161 injured. (NAVSEA DC Museum)

2.   This is a facetious remark made by Senator Obama a day later at the Al Smith dinner, in New York City, which also was attended by Senator McCain. It was one of Senator Obama's "stand up" comedy remarks of the night, joking about the characterization as "that one" that Senator McCain used when referring to Senator Obama during the second debate.

3.   It should be added that, afterwards, while reading the *Washington Post*, I found that E.J. Dionne, Jr. (Dionne 2008) also had highlighted this moment from the debate.

4.   By Election Day, Senator Obama had been endorsed by 287 (64 percent) newspapers vs. 159 (36 percent) for Senator McCain, with a 3:1 ratio in terms of circulation for Senator Obama, according to *Editor & Publisher*, a trade magazine for the newspaper industry (Mitchell/Hill 2008).

5.   In the end, an obvious believer in the role of a loyal opposition, Peggy Noonan did say that she would vote Republican (as she announced during *Morning Joe*). It is important, however, to underscore that even in the blue Northeast or the red South, an opposition vote does count, hopefully leading to a more intelligent loyal opposition.

9

An Outward Look

The Ugly American and the American Dream

October 21, 2008
"If you want to make peace, you don't talk to your friends. You talk to your enemies."
—*Moshe Dayan.*

The campaign season in its waning days has shown us a glimpse of an America I perhaps naively believed did not exist anymore. Is it really an undercurrent of American values or is it just the reflection of a vocal minority that brings back the haunting question, a bit changed now: "Are you now or have you ever been a member of a socialist movement? Do you know anyone who is or has been?" When Minnesota Rep. Michele Bachmann,[1] called on the media to expose who in Congress is pro-America and who is anti-America, was she really calling out for another HUAC (House Un-American Activities Committee), this time led by the likes of Sean Hannity and Rush Limbaugh?

The chilling message thread trend that the Republican campaign is using at this time is based on the divisive question: "Are you one of us?" "Is he one of us?" They call themselves "Great Americans" in a way that suggests a membership into some sort of exclusive club or elitist clan into which only a few are allowed. This divisive seed seems to be giving rise to a Republican Party fundamental—as phrased by President Bush's admonition in his September 2001 speech a shortly before the Afghanistan War and in a news conference in November—that others (countries in that case) are either with us or against us (CNN 2001, Bush 2001). In the case of this address, we were perhaps a little shocked by such blatant and extreme Manichaeism, but were tempered by the greater shock of the 9/11 events two months earlier.

The approach that seeks to make enemies out of people, parties, or even countries with dissenting views, however, distorts what America is all about. America is a land of democracy, opportunity, inclusiveness, and fairness. Democracy is about giving voice to dissension and about working together with opponents in order to achieve common goals. The real threat to democracy arises when factions driven by ambition use populist tactics of hate to create enemies for a final goal of division and conquest. These were the tactics used—thankfully unsuccessfully but with lingering consequences—in the 1950s by McCarthyites and in the 1960s by the likes of the Weather Underground and the Black Panthers.

The GOP has strayed, and I am afraid that this rising Republican philosophy has deviated from true conservative values regarding fiscal responsibility, government intrusion into private lives, and hard work as the basis of wealth creation for all. It is now a philosophy that pursues the conflicting goals of an aggressive military enforcing democracy—or U.S. interests—around the world on one hand, and the demagogical position of minimal taxation on the other hand—a tax policy that cannot support the armed forces required for an aggressive military position.[2] It is now a philosophy that says *"government, out of my way"* (Governor Palin during the October 8 VP debate), but wants to make sure that your private phone conversations can be monitored without a court order; not to mention the intrusion into the most difficult choice women are sometimes forced to make, as the choice of abortion is. It is now a philosophy that by applying "voodoo economics"—Bush, Sr.'s coinage during his primary against President Reagan—of trickle-down policy has presided over the greatest growth of income inequality that America has seen during the last eighty years—talk about redistribution of wealth![3]

I support Senator Obama for president, yes, and perhaps my opinions are tainted by this fact. But first and foremost, I support America and the American Dream of a fair society working together to advance opportunity for all within a civilized discourse. I do support fiscal responsibility, but I believe it cannot be based on tax time-shifting policies of "spend and borrow." I do support the right to privacy, and I do believe that it is possible that hard work can at least maintain your socio-economic status, and perhaps even raise it. What I cannot support is anyone who tries to divide us in order to win at all costs, leaving their own honor and principles behind, as regrettably it seems that the Republican Party and Senator McCain are doing. An Ugly America that I thought we had left behind has come back to haunt us.

The Latin America Trifecta: Brazil, Mexico, and Colombia

October 22, 2008

The Latin American continent is complex and evolving. As political institutions have evolved from their common origin, disparities have increased, impacting social and economic life differently. In the beginning most Latin American countries' constitutions were patterned after interpretations of the U.S. Constitution—as federated republics with a centralized representative body and an independent central executive power. These republics were patterned initially thus, as opposed to parliamentary systems with strong legislative bodies (though most former British colonies have governments based on the parliamentary system). In many cases, constitutions evolved after their first enactments and now include various systems of European-style proportional representation of political minorities through representatives-at-large, creating the basis for myriad parties with vocal representation in the deliberative bodies. The European influence of social-democratic political thought is common for most political tendencies in Latin America, with the usual variations to the right and to the left of this basic foundation of state interventionism—ranging from radical communism to Christian-democracy.

Among the major countries in Latin America, Brazil, Chile, Peru, and Argentina have runoff clauses in their electoral system, as well as Ecuador, whereas Venezuela, Colombia, and Mexico do not. In cases where no runoff elections are used as part of the electoral mechanism, and because of the multitude of fractious parties that often exist, presidents can and have been elected with just between 30 to 40 percent of the popular vote.[4] Under pluralistic systems constituted as these, it is a rarity when a president gets elected with more than 50 percent of the vote. Of those countries listed with runoffs, Argentina is unique in allowing victory with 45 percent of the vote or with 40 percent of the vote if the difference between the winner and the runner up is 10 percent or greater. Of additional interest is Bolivia with runoff elections by members of the parliament, as opposed to by popular vote.

The impact of having or not having runoffs can be significant politically. In 2006, for example, Peru held elections under their runoff system. The first round gave Lieutenant Colonel Ollanta Humala—a demagogue populist with Chávez /Morales-like rhetoric—a victory with 30.6 percent over his rival, Alan García—a more traditional centrist social-democrat—who obtained 24.3 percent of all valid votes. However, in the runoff García obtained 52.6 percent vs. 47.4 percent for Ollanta

Humala. The political landscape in Latin America would be quite different if the Chávez-supported Humala had won the presidency of Peru in 2006. Soon thereafter, Ecuador held elections in which the Chávez-supported candidate (Rafael Correa) lost in the first round, but prevailed in the second over a right of center pro-business industrialist with little popular sympathy.

Colonel Chávez's interference with the internal politics of Peru has been maintained over the years, supporting Lt. Col. Humala's factions with money and propaganda. For example, after the devastating Ica earthquake of August 15, 2007—which strength was 8.0 in the Richter scale—it was reported that food supplies with labels depicting Humala and Chávez were distributed in many areas with the message: "The Peruvian government acts in an inefficient, slow and heartless manner, notwithstanding the pain of the victims, leaving them to the mercy of hunger, thirst and delinquency" (Mcdonnell 2007).

Peru's recent history with extremism likely had an influence over the electorate and led to President García's victory. Voters maybe saw in Lt. Col. Humala a potentially divisive leader who could bring back the violence associated with the era of the Shining Path. The horrific violence enacted by this terrorist group was squelched with an equally extreme response by then President Alberto Fujimori. But the actions by Fujimori's government, contravening universal human rights and basic legal rights within Peru in order to defeat the Shining Path, have come back to haunt Mr. Fujimori and his close associates, now standing or having stood trial for these violations. Just as Abimael Guzman should be and is in jail for his heinous crimes against humanity, the fact that Peru recognizes that even against such terror presidents should act within the law is a civics lesson for the world.

As another example of the impact of having or not having runoffs, in Mexico's 2006 Presidential election, Felipe Calderón—of the right of center PAN (Partido de Acción Nacional) Party—prevailed with 35.59 percent of the votes, over his ideological opposite, Andrés Manuel López Obrador (candidate for PRD, Partido de la Revolución Democrática), who came in second with 35.31 percent. The situation left the country without a clear mandate or sense of ideological direction. While President Calderón has increased his popularity since the election, and López Obrador wasted his political capital in trying to shut down Mexico City for weeks on end, the circumstances of these elections left a lingering divisiveness that may still play out in the future.

The political stability of these countries clearly shifts with their electoral and representative systems, and that must be taken into account within any U.S. foreign policy formulation related to Latin America. While often in pluralistic elections the government is voted in by a minority of all voters, with the consequent problems brought about by a lack of a clear mandate, in runoff elections the rationalizing mind set of "voting against" or "choosing the lesser of two evils" is often the one that will likely be behind the victory by the prevailing candidate, leaving also a precariously based mandate. In the face of it, however, seemingly more legitimate.

My focus in this section is on countries that can and should be part of a concerted effort for active and positive engagement by the next administration. All countries signatories of the Pathway to Prosperity in the Americas Initiative[5] should obviously be part of this engagement, but I wish to zero in on what I call the Latin America Trifecta, a winning combination of key allies and clear leaders in the region: Brazil, Mexico, and Colombia. With a combined GDP of $2.4 trillion, this trio of countries represents the seventh largest economy in the world. Together, they are equal to the combined economies of the states of New York, Florida, and Illinois, and represent 72.7 percent of Latin America's GDP overall. In terms of population, they add up to 379.5 million inhabitants, or 66.6 percent of the population of Latin America. This is not to diminish the critical importance of other countries such as Peru, Chile, and others, struggling democracies that thrive in their strong mutual relationship with the U.S. It is by focusing on these three countries that the U.S., at this time, can strengthen its ties with all of Latin America, in essence by caring about and keeping promises with the whole region.

Brazil

Brazil is definitely the most powerful of all three countries in this trifecta. With a strong technological base—including a burgeoning space program, nuclear plants, a military and aviation industry that exports weapons and aircraft to other countries including the U.S.—Brazil has developed almost independently from the rest of the continent. Isolated by language and an immense jungle, the Brazilian people have created a major country almost on their own. The diversity of major Brazilian industries includes leather processing, high fashion and quality clothes' manufacturing and design, automobiles, as well as agro technologies pioneering, for example, the wide use of ethanol based fuels. A diversified agriculture has also boomed in Brazil, with new major crops in maize, soybean, rice, wheat, others and, of course, coffee, driving a major export sector in this area (Vistesen 2008). As in most Latin American countries, Brazil had a period of repressive regimes that tore its civil society and sowed the seeds of the great income inequality existing in this country (Freire 1996). With a Gini coefficient[6] of 0.57, its income inequality is among the highest in the region. Brazil is successfully addressing income inequality through government policy tools and initiatives: it is estimated that the top 10 percent of the country's inhabitants obtained a 51.3 percent share of the national income or consumption in 1993 (Freire 1996), and, as indicated in the most recent UN Human Development Report, in 2004 44.8 percent share of income or consumption was for the top 10 percent of the population. By way of contrast, for the U.S. this measure is 29.9, Mexico's is 39.4, and Colombia's is 46.9 percent (United Nations Development Programme 2007/2008). This inequality is the major source of Brazil's political turmoil and social tension, and—while it seemed to have been used as political fodder by President Luiz Inácio Lula da Silva in his original campaign—it could still be used by other populists and demagogues for their own political ambition, by stirring divisiveness and social unrest. President Lula has tried to continue to diminish this income distribution inequality with a certain degree of success. An article in the *New York Times* on July 2008 reports as follows (Barrionuevo 2008):

> Long famous for its unequal distribution of wealth, Brazil has shrunk its income gap by six percentage points since 2001, more than any other country in South America this decade, said Francisco Ferreira, a lead economist at the World Bank. While the top 10 percent of Brazil's earners saw their cumulative income rise by 7 percent from 2001 to 2006, the bottom 10 percent shot up by 58 percent, according to Marcelo Côrtes Neri, the director of the Center for Social Policies at the Getulio Vargas Foundation in Rio de Janeiro. But Brazil is also outspending most of its neighbors on social programs, and overall public spending continues to be nearly four times as high as what Mexico spends as a percentage of its gross national product, Mr. Ferreira said.

The social unrest associated with income inequalities translates into general personal insecurity and into the violence of gang-riddled *favelas* around Brazil. In order to address the core issue of inequality the government seems to be using a funds transfer policy (Barrionuevo 2008), and utilizing the tools of micro-banking and mini-enterprise funding as part of Brazil's government policy aimed to diminish income inequality. As an intrinsic part of these social improvements, Brazil has also worked on increasing its literacy rate. Though the latest numbers in the UN HDR (United Nations Development Programme 2007/2008) do not have a timeline comparison for literacy among adults, the results of these programs can be seen when comparing the gaps in the age demographics: youth literacy rate (ages 15-24) is 96.8 percent, while adult literacy (ages 15 and older) was 88.6 percent. The comparables for Mexico and Colombia are 97.6 youth / 91.6 percent adult, and 98.0 youth / 92.8 percent adult, respectively (United Nations Development Programme 2007/2008).

The obvious identified mutual interests between Brazil and the US include increased cooperation in aerospace and military technology development, control of nuclear proliferation and energy sector development—including oil and alternate fuels as well. Special care should be considered regarding the sensitive issue of agricultural commodities' trade. These primary commercial interests will be supported by the other key common interest: regional stability. For this interest, the issue of income inequality and social redress is paramount in order to avoid the demagoguery that has plagued Brazil's neighboring countries, Argentina and Venezuela. The U.S. should support by word and by action Brazil's policies that are helping to decrease social inequality through the mini-enterprise, financial educational and, literacy programs already in place.

Mexico

Mexico is the second leg in Latin America's triad that the U.S. needs for strengthening its hemispheric position. Income distribution in this country is also a significant issue, but with a Gini coefficient of 0.461, sixteenth in the region, it is not as negative as Brazil's but indicative of inequality nonetheless. Just like in the case of Brazil, the social pressure created by this inequality creates conditions conducive to populism and demagoguery. But in fact, Mexico's Gini coefficient has decreased from approximately 0.50 in 1990 to its current level. This decrease has been probably been driven by the NAFTA effect and by a political transformation that has transitioned Mexico from de facto one-party rule to a more pluralistic system.[7] The standard of living for Mexican workers has increased, led by an industrial and economic policy that recognizes that the oil industry is not growing and that diversification is required.

The greatest pains in this transition to a more modern society have been those related to the stronghold and influence of the drug cartels, which are very feudal gangs in composition. From the everyday schoolyard to the police station to the Justice Ministry, the drug cartels have insidiously infiltrated everyday life throughout Mexico. President Calderón has made a successful effort to combat this infiltration, bringing in the armed forces to substitute police efforts, in a real "war on drugs" with a consequent dramatic and bloody vengeance by these cartels (Ellingwood 2008).[8]

Mexico is a country rightly proud of its rich ancestry and its cultural and racial heritage, and looks forward towards building a better society upon its own roots. Major industries that have diversified away from the primary (mining and agriculture) sector include, among others, Maquila, mobile communications, and TV and movie production. The battle against corruption in the judicial system and law enforcement institutions continues. The extent to which the rule of law is strong in a given society is an index of development, and Mexico is fighting hard to increase its social, civil, and criminal rule of law.

The U.S. has to ensure the establishment of a domestic drug policy that is effective in further reducing the power of the Mexican drug cartels, and this would be a supportive step in the painful effort that Mexico itself is enduring due to the effects of drug trafficking. The critical issues to address as related to investment policy and cooperation between the U.S. and Mexico are NAFTA and a comprehensive revision of this treaty (see section below: Free Trade and Supranational Market Failures), joint oil and energy policies within the context of a new U.S. energy policy initiative, and immigration controls.

Colombia

In conversations with Colombians today, the most striking development over the last few years has been the coalescing of a national identity. This is sometimes taken for granted for any nation and yet in Latin America, with uncharacteristically stable borders over the last 200 years, this has not been a clearly identifiable issue. Except for the recent case of Bolivia,[9] there had not been a credible threat of breakaway provinces or territories since Panama gained full independence from Colombia over 100 years ago in 1903, under the aegis of President Theodore Roosevelt in his quest to build the Canal.

But in many countries there is a dearth of national identity brought about by degrees of ethnic differences—Chiapas in Mexico and Bolivia are standout examples—and economic regional differences, with their consequent inequalities (for example Zulia state in Venezuela and, once again Bolivia). The socioeconomic forces working against national identity are reinforced by physical conditions such as poor transportation infrastructure, urban polarization, and geographical barriers such as mountains, jungles, and swamps.

In Colombia, though, the struggle that civil society has had against the drug cartels, the various rebel forces, and their alliances, has unified the country against violence and lawlessness. This violence at its peak led to the assassination of presidential candidate Luis Carlos Galán, an event that, combined with the bombing of Avianca's flight 203,[10] was the turning point for the country against the violence of the drug cartels.

This backlash, however had the nefarious consequence of eventually spawning the AUC.[11] As the drug cartels were prosecuted more vigorously, strong alliances of convenience between these and the long-standing guerrilla movements appeared, which had dabbled with "drug taxes" for a while but now got directly involved in production and trafficking. These combined forces, creating new funding sources and structure, now engaged the guerrillas directly in outright criminal activity; the social backlash against the drug cartels now spilled over against the insurgent guerrillas. In 1997 the AUC was formed in response to the growing power and lawlessness of the drug/guerrilla combination, and the weakness of the central government's response. However, as a vigilante group acting outside the law shortly thereafter the AUC saw its own convenience in associating with the drug trade in order to achieve funding, and became one more group trying to control territories and drug trafficking.

The roots of the long continuing guerrilla warfare can be traced once again to one of the largest income distribution inequality in the Americas and rooted in the history of armed social conflict between the "Conservative" and the "Liberal" historical political parties of Colombia in the 1950s. With a current Gini coefficient of 0.586, Colombia is only surpassed by Bolivia (0.601)—a historically and notoriously poor country with a fifth of the population of Colombia, less than 10 million inhabitants (smaller than, say, New York City)—and Haiti (Gini 0.592).

The original FARC and ELN (Ejército de Liberación Nacional) guerrilla movements were ideologically driven and started in the early 1960s at the time the Castro regime was trying to "export" its revolution. Cuba in fact recognized the guerrilla movements as "belligerent forces" many years ago, and as recently as January 2008, Venezuela's Chávez did the same for the FARC, and called for many other countries to do so.

When current President Alvaro Uribe's predecessor Andrés Pastrana (1998-2002) granted a safe-haven territory to the leftist guerrilla movements, essentially "without preconditions," he set himself up for a political dead end, ineffectively dealing with the guerrilla/drug forces and their social backlash. In a territory larger than Switzerland the guerrillas were able to organize, recruit and strengthen, and set up drug factories, training camps and kidnap farms. Campaigning against this policy and his continued hard line against guerrilla appeasement has garnered President

Uribe the highest popularity of any president in the country's history, leading first to his reelection and now for calls of constitutional reform to allow him a third term. His message of nationalism, civil order, and rule of law has resonated and driven a new sense of pride among law-abiding Colombians.

The history of criminal and social violence in Colombia is gruesome, but all facts lead us to believe that a stronger civil society is addressing the issue from a legal standpoint: major violence indicators such as number of kidnappings and murders have decreased over the last few years; politicians and industrialists associated with paramilitary (AUC) operations are being investigated, arrested, and convicted; and there is an increase in purges of armed forces and police inflicting violence upon civilian population and violating human rights. It is to be noted that major opposition to the U.S./Colombia Free Trade Agreement has centered on paramilitary (AUC) actions and government response to the human rights violations by this group, but scarcely mention the effect of leftist guerrilla forces, their terrorist tactics, and their association with drug trafficking. To be a trade unionist in Colombia is hazardous, indeed, but the seemingly good faith effort of the current government to demobilize paramilitaries and prosecute union killing cases has brought down the violence, from over 200 a year to less than half of that, and an increasing rate of convictions.

It is in the interest of the United States to assist Colombia in three major areas: economic opportunity, drug trafficking control, and demobilization and assimilation of paramilitaries and guerrillas. Economic opportunity should be motivated by addressing income inequality, clearly based on a fair Free Trade Agreement that rewards Colombia's efforts to establish due process and rule of law. Economic opportunity between the U.S. and Colombia should allow trade opportunities for medium-sized and non-traditional businesses, while at the same time strengthening Colombia's traditional industries: publishing and media, agricultural commodities, and textiles and apparel.

Control of the drug trade—the underlying root of Colombia's criminal violence and corruption—requires, as in the case of Mexico, a new outlook on the part of U.S. domestic policies regarding drug consumption, treatment and trafficking. The support of the military's counterterrorist and anti drug production campaign in the Colombian countryside should be continued—albeit recognizing and supporting the continued prosecution of human rights violations and addressing crimes perpetrated against human rights—at the same time as the demobilization and assimilation of paramilitaries and guerrillas: a segment of society that needs to be reconciled within a nation ruled by law.

As in all the countries singled out in this discussion, for Colombia the strengthening of the judiciary and the increased belief in the existence of a predictable, reliable and fair justice system through the rule of law has benefited society. Addressing issues of income inequality, either by direct transfers or greater economic opportunity, alleviates social tensions that give rise to the insidious populism and divisiveness, which in turn leads to social disenfranchisement, civil violence, and the concentration of power in the hands of a few—as in the historical case of Venezuela, and with the consequences in such case. It is in supporting measures that address these inequality issues that the U.S. can exert a positive influence, including, but by no means limited to, trade and mutual cooperation agreements that contemplate opportunities for the working and emerging middle class in these countries.

Free Trade and Supranational Market Failures

October 30, 2008

Free trade seeks to allow efficient allocation of productive resources by making the region with the greatest comparative advantage in the extraction, production, or distribution of a particular good, the one that supplies such good at the lowest price to the end consumer. Proponents of unrestricted free trade are driven by the expectation that free markets regulate themselves and allocate all resources efficiently. If, in international contexts, free trade agreements were in fact instruments for an extension of perfect free markets, it is possible that such trade would be self-regulated and revert to an efficient distribution of resources.

International trade, however, is regularly conducted through a great number of imperfect layers, the most obvious ones being the tariffs placed by importer nations on goods from other countries. Other such layers include non-tariff barriers such as subsidies and price supports on local products, legal restrictions such as health regulations, labeling, accessibility or usage, trademarks, copyrights and patents, moral content, etc., technical compatibility (voltage, hardware metrics, etc.), and currency transfer logistics.

The maze of paperwork involved in a simple export or import transaction is a barrier just by itself, not to mention coordinating the exchange of compensation from one country to another between the parties involved. Thus the promise to assist or facilitate these transactions in order to participate in seemingly attractive markets is the tantalizing promise dangled when the prospect of a Free Trade Agreement with any nation or regional block is offered.

The North America Free Trade Agreement (NAFTA) can be evaluated as the first truly modern commercial treaty of this era, and some lessons can be extracted from its history and effects. NAFTA did not create a "sucking sound" of jobs going South of the Border, as Ross Perot suggested it would.[12] In fact, it created jobs on both sides, within the major industries it was primarily focused on: automotive and maquila, and agriculture and financial services. The actual numbers and accounting tend to be skewed in favor by whoever is making the argument. For example, Robert E. Scott calculated in 2003 that approximately 880,000 jobs had been lost to NAFTA based on his analysis of jobs gains and losses in import and export in affected sectors (Scott 2003). He himself, though, admits the difficulty in estimating these numbers, in particular as to the assignment of multipliers (jobs affected by each job loss or gain) and as to the attribution of gains/losses across regions, be they states or countries (Scott 2003: Appendix 1 and note 8). His argument is strong regarding total job loss in the period studied, but to attribute all job losses he accounts for (based on imports) only to NAFTA would give this sole market factor element a greater significance than it may have. Unfortunately for his original argument, ceteres paribus [all else being equal] is as real as Utopia.

The period studied by Dr. Scott includes the consequences and restructurings brought by the 1991-92 recession. As the productive base in the U.S. was transformed, the greatest threat to manufacturing lower skilled jobs became China,[13] which took full advantage, starting in 1994,[14] of its MFN status.[15] Between 1990 and 1993 Chinese investment in Mexico itself increased, anticipating NAFTA.[16] After China's MFN was renewed unconditionally on May 26, 1994 and ushering in Clinton's special relationship with China, the Mexico option for foreign direct investment (from China and others) began to lose importance, with China on a fast track towards full incorporation into the world economy (Fung, KC et al. 2005). It was reported at the time that retailers and manufacturers (groups united under the umbrella organization Business Coalition for U.S.-China Trade, among other China lobbying firms and in addition to such groups as the National Association of Manufacturers) in particular were pleased with the normalization of trade relations with China (Markowitz 1994, Hall 1997, Magnusson 1997). China was a cheaper alternative to Mexico, despite the increased transportation costs and in spite of the NAFTA agreements. On October 10, 2000 President Clinton signed into law the bill granting PNTR to China; effective December 2001, China was granted PNTR and eventual WTO membership in December 2002 allowing China's full incorporation into world commerce, based on the minimum standard of free open trade between all countries.

In evaluating the consequences of unfettered trade with China, it can be argued at this time that Wal-Mart could be singled out as the largest destroyer of small manufacturing jobs in America, because most of its supplier base shifted to China as a consequence of Wal-Mart's corporate policies (Fishman 2003), as MFN took hold. Now this company, the largest in the U.S., has become structurally vulnerable to the currency pressures on the Chinese yuan. External pressures on China's currency exchange policy can be documented at least as early as 1994 (Jisi et al. 1994, *China Daily News* 2006), but domestic pressures on its currency within China itself will increase as imported products become more expensive. In order to increase the standard of living, as China stimulates its economy with its own economic package, and as middle- and privileged-class consumers increase internal demand, it is likely that a more liberal currency exchange policy will be allowed to lower the local prices of imported goods as a counter inflation measure.

The net effect of NAFTA is thus not clear, but it is hard to argue that the China effect, which has no special trade treaty with the U.S., has been devastating. It is estimated that China's exports to the U.S. were $120 billion in 2002, mostly in manufactured goods, while the exports from Canada and Mexico into the U.S., according to Dr. Scott's figures, were $85 billion, including oil imports (the U.S. imported about 32.2 percent of its total oil imports from those two countries in 2002).[17] Scott himself recognizes this in his later research on the issue, attributing to China a greater impact on job losses (Scott, R. 2008), and estimating a total loss of 2.3 million jobs, due to the structure of trade with China.

So, if the impact on U.S. jobs and the global environment which were attempted to be neutralized with the NAFTA supplemental agreements was still felt by simply shifting trade to China and away from NAFTA, what shall we make of the need or not of specific trade agreements between nations? It seems that free market rules have applied more to China than to Mexico or Canada in the import/export relationship with the U.S. Trade agreements have become, then, the de facto regulators of unfettered free markets in an international context, laying down rules of trade and business that can and do affect policy directly. It is when no specific trade agreement exists that unregulated free markets in a global economy can have greater negative consequences and result in "unfair trade."

Trade Agreements and Fair Trade

A few years ago we saw many public demonstrations against multilateral organization meetings throughout the world, including at the start of the WTO Doha Round in Seattle, at gatherings such as the World Economic Forum in Davos, the G8, and others.[18] The core complaint behind these protests was that structured and unstructured non-governmental organizations (NGOs) and other stakeholders were being left out of these multilateral meetings, and decisions on the economic and regulatory framework of globalization were being made that affected them. The call was for "fair trade" as opposed to free trade, suggesting that there were affected parties not participating in the drafting of international trade and commerce rules, agreements and decisions, and thus getting unfavorable treatment. The drafting of these treaties now includes (or attempts to include) issues affecting these organizations and groups, not as addenda or supplements (as in NAFTA), but as part and parcel of the body of the agreements.

We have come a long way from NAFTA and from Seattle. It is clear now that as multinational corporations seek to shift assets, transfer costs, and seek minimum compliance to maximize profits (as any self respecting corporation should and must do in order to survive within a capitalist environment), supranational oversight of operations is required in order to balance corporate operations with the negative externalities created.[19] Because these corporations operate in environments with multiple legal and business regulations, it is natural for them to pursue the minimum required compliance in a juggling act of economic factors that structures operations so that profits are maximized: labor replaces capital where labor is cheapest and unregulated; profits are transferred to the least taxed location[20]; and capital will be invested in the least regulated business environment—depending for this additionally on infrastructure and security, and investment protection and incentives. With the expected rise in energy and transportation costs, location to market also becomes a great factor now.

Because of the potential of runaway negative externalities in an unregulated global business environment, the intervention and protests have led labor organizations, environmental groups, and others to attempt to participate actively in the drafting of the treaties to counteract the effects of globalization of business. The 2009 World Economic Forum at Davos, for example, lists in its agenda great participation by these groups, including NGOs, trade unions, science, religion, sports, and cultural representatives. It is paramount and part of the advancement of nations, that these trade treaties and other rules of international business address these factors and these stakeholders. A balanced regulatory framework that encourages business by decreasing economic barriers between markets but attempts to minimize the potential for negative externalities will create a positive growth environment in the long term for all nations involved.

It is within this context that Senator Obama's comments regarding NAFTA and the Colombia FTA during the campaign season should be viewed. The economy has changed, globalization has increased, and recognition of increasing interdependency and negative externalities make a review and revision of NAFTA appropriate at this time. It is not an abrogation that is called for, but after nearly fifteen years, a major revision and update should not be seen as unusual. As regards to Colombia, the agreement should preferably be approved expeditiously, as it will open markets for the U.S.—reciprocating the openness that U.S. markets already have for Colombia—and send an encouraging signal to a key ally in Latin America. However, given the Bush administration's penchant for lax control and regulation, a review focusing on issues such as those raised in this essay should be conducted, and supplemental agreements such as were done for NAFTA may be called for. In essence a new way to look at Trade Treaties, focusing on positive and negative externalities for all stakeholders involved.[21]

Notes

1.   Congresswoman Bachmann (R-MN) said on *Hardball*, with Chris Matthews on October 17 2008: "I wish the American media would take a great look at the views of the people in Congress and find out, are they pro-America or anti-America? I think people would love to see an expose like that" (Bachmann 2008). She was reelected with 46.4 percent of the votes vs. 43.4 percent obtained by her Democratic opponent, Elwyn Tinklenberg, in a three-way race for the Minnesota 6th congressional district seat.
2.   "War on the Cheap" according to Secretary Rumsfeld, as reported in 2003 (BBC News 2003) and a policy espoused by the likes of "Joe the Plumber."
3.   In measures of income inequality, the United States' trend is towards a rise in inequality over the last twenty years. In fact, at this time income inequality is trending to be greater in the U.S. than Mexico, where the trend has been towards a decrease over the last ten years.
4.   In a notable example, Rafael Caldera was elected president of Venezuela in 1968 with less than 29 percent of the popular vote.
5.   The signatory countries of The Pathway for Prosperity of the Americas Initiative are Canada, Chile, Colombia, Costa Rica, Dominican Republic, El Salvador, Guatemala, Honduras, Mexico, Panama, Peru and the United States (White House Press Release 2008).

6.   The Gini coefficient is a statistical measure of inequality in income distribution, where 0 indicates perfect distribution of income (everybody has the same income) and 1 is extreme inequality in the distribution of income (one person has all the income). Extreme ranges are Denmark, with a Gini coefficient of approximately 0.247, and Namibia, with a Gini coefficient of 0.743 (UNDP 2007/2008). Most developed countries with a sizable GDP range between 0.24 and 0.36. The US Gini coefficient is approximately 0.408 (United Nations Development Programme 2007/2008). Furthermore, since this measure started being used by economists in 1967, the US Gini coefficient has gone up, from 0.397 in 1968 to 0.463 in 2007. Gini coefficients in this essay are from United Nations Development Programme (2007/2008) unless otherwise noted.

7.   On July 2, 2000, Vicente Fox won the Mexico general election with 42.52 percent of the vote, over his closest rival Francisco Labastida of the PRI, who garnered 36.11 percent of the vote. This marked the end of PRI's (Partido Revolucionario Institucional) stronghold on the presidency since 1910, in a system that in effect had instituted presidential succession based on the designation by the office holder from one president to the next, blatantly buying and brokering votes to ensure continuity in power.

8.   The *Los Angeles Times* has an informative and dramatic continuing series called "Mexico Under Siege: The Drug War at our Doorstep" with a number of articles on a timeline starting in June 3, 2008 with the article in reference, to this day. In a "body count clock" it is estimated that since January 2007 more than 6,000 people have been killed in drug related deaths. That is a greater number than the U.S. casualties since the war in Iraq began, which is over 4,000 according to the Associated Press count (*Los Angeles Times* 2007/09).

9.   In 2006 and 2007 the pressures for autonomy or outright independence from the capital provinces by the "Half Moon" provinces of Santa Santa Cruz, Beni, Pando, and Tarija, comprising the richest regions in the country was at its peak. Business and civic groups from this region were opposed to reformist measures enacted by President Evo Morales (beginning with the nationalization of major extractive industries in the region, (Carl T., D. Keane 2007) and the president's proposed new constitution, and exacerbated by the ethnic differences of the majority ethnic Indians, mostly poor, and the minority non-Indian, which is not. After bloody clashes, boycotts and protests, a compromise on constitutional reforms was achieved and these separatist forces, for now, seem to have calmed down.

10.   On November 27, 1989 Avianca flight 203 exploded in midair a few minutes after takeoff from Bogotá en route to Cali. Over 100 people died in this attack for which the notorious Pablo Escobar, head of the Medellín drug cartel, claimed responsibility. The attack was directed against the leading presidential candidate at the time Cesar Gaviria, who had not boarded the plane and went on to become president from 1990 to 1994. Pablo Escobar was killed in 1993 by an anti-drug police task force while trying to avoid capture. In *Killing Pablo* author Mark Bowden estimates that over 4,000 deaths are directly attributable to Escobar.

11.   Autodefensas Unidas de Colombia, a paramilitary organization associated with conservative forces of Colombia, in particular landowners in lawless regions of the country.

12.   Said during Ross Perot's presidential campaign in the second televised debate against George H.W. Bush and Bill Clinton on October 15, 1992. His actual quote in that instance was "There will be a job-sucking sound going south.," which he developed for the third debate (October 19, 1992) as "...You implement that NAFTA, the Mexican trade agreement, where they pay people a dollar an hour,

have no health care, no retirement, no pollution controls, et cetera, et cetera, et cetera, and you're going to hear a giant sucking sound of jobs being pulled out of this country."

13. According to a recent study, while Chinese imports increased nearly twenty times between 1979 and 1989, mean wages for high school graduate level workers in manufacturing sectors impacted by these imports decreased 9.25 percent in the same period (Kandilov 2008).

14. This was the beginning of the end run in terms of China's entry as a full-fledged player in the international economic scene. In 2001 China was accepted into the World Trade Organization (WTO), in effect ending the need for annual Most Favored Nation (MFN) status renewals. Despite its WTO membership, China has been accused of manipulating its currency in order to maintain its costs low and an international competitive advantage (Jisi et al. 1994, Scott 2008b).

15. Most Favored Nation or MFN is perhaps a misnomer. It basically refers to treating a country the same as any other member of the WTO (previously, the signatories to the General Agreement on Trade and Tariffs, GATT). Only eight nations did not have MFN status with America at the time of China being granted permanent MFN by the US in 1999. In 1998 the term MFN was changed to PNTR, or Permanent Normal Trade Relations. By taking the words "Most Favored Nation" out of the concept, it became politically more palatable to grant such status to China.

16. At the time I was very involved with Mexico and its business community, and it was clear to me how China, as well as other countries, were attempting to hedge their bets by increasing their capital investments in Mexico.

17. U.S. Energy Information Administration (EIA), U.S. Imports of Oil by Country of Origin. Approximately $27 billion at the time.

18. Billed as "Anti-Globalization" protests these have included Seattle, WTO/Doha 1999, G8 1999 (Köln) and 2008 (Hokkaido), and WEF Davos, 2000 to 2003 among others.

19. A negative externality is a market failure whereby the full cost of a decision or action is not borne by the individual who makes that decision or carries out that action, shifting that cost to others, typically society at large. Noise pollution is a typical example of a negative externality.

20. Despite the existence of International Accounting Standards Board (IASB) and Financial Accounting Standards Board (FASB) rulings that seek to address this issue, this is an area that all corporations try to address utilizing transfer pricing and double taxation to its maximum advantage (and have a right to under current regulation and market rules).

21. Moisés Naím, Chief Editor of *Foreign Policy Magazine*, in a recent article addresses the regulation of the naturally increased flow of goods between international markets brought about by modern commerce, including the basics, such as the mutual benefits of lowered trade barriers, to more complex issues such as oversight of product quality. As to this last point he states: "No country acting alone stands as good a chance of monitoring and curtailing such lethal goods [such as deadly pet food and poisoned toothpaste] as does the WTO working in concert with governments across the globe" [my insert] (Naím 2007). As an example, the consequences of the *Consumer Product Safety Improvement Act of 2008*, in effect a trade barrier passed by the US Congress in response to the China products scare of 2008, are not fully played out yet but it is potentially foreseeable that some US costume jewelry manufacturers using Austrian crystals could go out of business, or that Goodwill stores could be threatened with criminal prosecution for reselling untested articles of clothing with undetermined lead content in their zippers.

10

The Elections

Election Week

November 5, 2008

On a beautiful Florida Fall day, exactly one week before Election Day, and taking advantage of "early voting," I voted. There were around five hundred people in the poll line—about the same amount as the margin by which Al Gore lost the state of Florida and the general election in 2000—and most were in a festive, patient mood. There were some activists, and some high schoolers—part of a civics program, busing high school kids to vote—listening as the ballot was explained to them. I spoke with some of these young voters; most of them, apparently, had the intention to vote for Senator Obama. There were a little less than a dozen kids—from a high school that I know has three thousand plus students—so I asked them if there were more buses coming, or had come a previous day, to which I was told that no, that was it for the school. Surprised, I was told by these kids that many others had not found about this "field trip," or simply did not care to go, perhaps planning to go on Election Day. Maybe these young slackers—taking the day off from school, indeed!— will motivate the others to go and vote, I thought. Oh, well...

Dr. Brenda Snipes, the Broward County supervisor of elections, was at my poll place—supervising. I struck up a conversation with her, and she told me that early turnout was very high and lines were long, yes, but on Election Day she expected that with more than forty times the voting places open (from 17 to 793), and with more than 20 percent of the vote already in through early elections, she did not foresee a problem. The next day, anyway, Governor Charlie Crist extended voting hours from eight to twelve hours, citing a "state emergency" (Florida Governor Executive Order 08-217). In fact there were no major problems on November 4 as far as access to the polls, and total turnout was estimated to be over 70 percent in Broward County Florida.

Nationally speaking, voting was a weeks-long process, as opposed to an Election Day event. Given the historical reasons for not voting (see below), the longer process must have definitely encouraged more people to go and vote, resulting in a larger turnout. Between absentee balloting and early voting, millions of people, more than ever before, voted before Election Day[1]; more than thirty states received approximately a quarter or a third of their registered voter's votes. In Florida, it was estimated that about 30 percent of registered voters had voted by the time early voting closed on Sunday, November 2, including all absentee ballots which had until Tuesday to arrive (MacDonald 2008). My sister, who lives in Seattle, reported to me that in Washington State nearly 90 percent of votes were sent in by mail, a fact difficult to check easily, but probably correct, seeing that out of thirty-nine counties in that state *only two do not exclusively* vote by mail.

As election eve lurks in my mind, a dread overcomes me. What if Obama Californians decide that they do not have to vote? After all, they are in an overwhelmingly "blue" state and on the east coast they have the election all wrapped up, they may think. As cable channels say they expect to have results and projections by 7:00 to 8:00 PM Eastern Time, it is a terrible thought on my mind: that expectations will trump action, and that the election will result in an incredible upset, giving the victory to the McCain/Palin ticket. Jitters abound, and (not so) unrealistic fears regarding the west coast make me think these rambling thoughts, that perhaps throw a smidgen of insight into some strategic thought by the Republicans.[2]

In a cynical epiphany, I understand this may be the reason why the Republicans are having major get-out-the-vote drives. While common wisdom says that low turnout typically and historically favors Republicans, in this case the partisan operatives are trying to convince supporters that, despite all the polling numbers and data, there is a chance to win this election by barely squeezing slim majorities in crucial states that could give the Republican ticket an Electoral College victory—popular vote notwithstanding—especially if the Democrats get overconfident. The Republican campaign's message is "go vote – we still have a chance!" Indeed, at this point it is complacency on the part of the Democrats what threatens the election victory, as Senator Obama has aptly said "snatching defeat from the jaws of victory." So, the Democratic campaign's message is "go vote – don't take victory for granted!" Who will win the turnout wars? Stay tuned…

But why, when, and how did turnout of voters become such a tool to manipulate representation? Is it not the civic duty and responsibility of every citizen to cast a vote in order to select leaders by democratic means, what this country is all about? Is that not the reason given for so much blood sacrifice through the ages, starting with the American Revolution? Or was the blood of our fathers spilt just to have a right we opt not to use because of inconvenience? Is it not the reason why my uncle fought with glory in the Battle of the Bulge and was awarded the Purple Heart?

According to the U.S. Census Bureau (see appendix 2) out of an eligible population of 215.6 million voters, only 125.7 million voted in 2004. That is 58.3 percent of all potential voters. That means that the votes with which President Bush was elected—62 million votes—represented only 28.8 percent of all citizens of voting age. And that election was an improvement regarding voters' turnout. In 2000, only 54.7 percent of potential voters came out, and in 1996, the percentage was 54.2 (Holder 2006).[3] So the tendency is moving in the right direction, but a big hurdle in representation still exists. What do the candidates' actions and strategies tell us about their commitment to have all eligible citizens vote?

The profile of the *registered voter* differs from that of the *non-registered voter*: the former is likely more affluent, white, older, and a long-time resident of the community; the latter is likely Hispanic, younger, with very low income and a newcomer to his/her community (Holder 2006). Voter registration drives are obviously directed to the unregistered, but the issue is that Republican strategists deem these drives to be more likely to lead into Democratic votes, given the demographics. That is why they decry all the registration hoopla by community organizers such as ACORN (Gordon 2008). The massive registration drives conducted during this campaign would seem to corroborate the Republican expectations, as the increase in Democratic Party enrollment was substantial in every state (Nicholas 2008).

On the other hand, the *registered non-voter*—likely to be white, between twenty-five to sixty-four years of age, maybe a woman from the south—has reasons not to vote that relate more to the way we vote than to their own disinterest or skepticism. Only 20 percent fall under the category *"not interested in politics/does not like any candidate."* Given registered non-voters demographics, it makes sense to have Governor Palin making the rounds down south to get out the vote at the end of the campaign, and for Governor Crist to have extended the hours of early voting in Florida. These non-voters are likely Republican. Hence, Republicans want to fire them up, motivate them, and give them many opportunities to go to the polls. These non-voters can make a substantial difference in the end.

Election Night

As I left work, around 7:00 PM, I looked up to the sky: there is a bright, waxing moon, almost smiling at us and, in perfect line with it, in conjunction, two bright objects—planets obviously—one of them I think is Venus or Jupiter, and the other is definitely Mars, with its reddish tinge. I am not superstitious by nature but find this spectacle in the nightly sky somewhat beautiful and disconcerting at the same time on this Election Day night.

The night unfolds, state polls close and, as returns start coming in, it seems obvious that Senator Obama is winning. In areas and states where he loses, he is close. In the greatest of the swing states, Florida, he takes an early lead that he maintains all night, though the networks are reluctant to call the state for him—pangs of 2000 anyone? Shortly after 11:00 PM EST it is over: Virginia is called by the networks, and Senator McCain has already lost Ohio and Pennsylvania; he telephones Senator Obama to concede. President Bush calls Senator Obama shortly thereafter and tells him: "What an awesome night for you. I promise to make this a smooth transition. You are about to go on one of the great journeys of life. Congratulations and go enjoy yourself" (Feller 2008). Always with his special way with words, always self-centered.

In the conclusion of a remarkable campaign, Senator Obama is poised to obtain at least 349 electoral votes, possibly more than 360 and over 51 percent, maybe 52 percent of the popular vote. The only possibly contested election, if the Republicans want to fight, is Indiana where Senator Obama wins by less than 1 percent of the vote.

Wednesday, November 5

Another morning seemingly like any other day: get up, feed the cats, get ready for work. This is, however, not just any other day. The trash needs to be taken out, and as I do so, change is in the air. America will never be the same, and as reactions from the world pour in, the monumentality of what has happened may begin to dawn on the recalcitrant few that have failed to recognize it yet. Forty years ago, in *Meet the Press*, RFK said in a prophetic way, "things are moving so fast in race relations a Negro could be president in 40 years." But Senator Obama's victory goes beyond the myopic perspective offered by Senator McCain in his concession speech regarding this moment as a great one for African

Americans.[4] While not minimizing this milestone for African Americans, this is America's moment, for all Americans, standing proud in the ideals of democracy and opportunity, and inspiring the rest of the world as a beacon of these ideals and what they represent.

Some TV commentators were asking, "If Senator McCain had won, would it mean that America is a racist country?" The answer to this question is a resounding *yes*. Senator Obama won because he ran a superb, nearly flawless campaign. His organization, message, consistency and energy led him to victory. He worked very hard for it and deserved to win. He was the best candidate. If Senator Obama were white, he would have won with probably less than half the effort. As Ralph Nader unequivocally stated early in the campaign, this was an election for the Democrats to lose (Nader 2008). Only in a year in which the Republican-led government demonstrated abysmal blunders in judgment, leadership, and administration, and a year in which the economy "cratered" spectacularly five weeks before the election, could the rejection of the party in power overcome the underlying racism in a segment of the population—a segment large enough that almost made the party in opposition lose the election. And, if left unchecked, that same segment will second guess to paralysis every move by President Obama's government, trying to deny him a second term.

For now though, there has been a change in America and, I believe, for the better. But it is just the beginning. President Elect Obama's speech in Chicago's Grant Park synthesizes this thought: "The road ahead will be long. Our climb will be steep. We may not get there in one year or even one term, but America—I have never been more hopeful than I am tonight that we will get there. I promise you—we as a people will get there."

And he promises sacrifice and hard work: "There will be setbacks and false starts. There are many who won't agree with every decision or policy I make as President, and we know that government can't solve every problem. But I will always be honest with you about the challenges we face. I will listen to you, especially when we disagree. And above all, I will ask you join in the work of remaking this nation the only way it's been done in America for two-hundred and twenty-one years—block by block, brick by brick, calloused hand by calloused hand."

Watching Senator Obama's campaign unfold over the last few months has been like listening to the unrelenting refrain of Ravel's *Bolero*, starting barely perceptible with a constant tune reiterated over and over with little variation, incorporating gradually new instruments into the march-like quality of the theme, adding richness to the experience, and finally finishing with a loud triumphant flourish. His character went on display during election season, changing from an expectation that maybe he was just a charming self-interested petty politician with a pretty speech—and waiting for the "Barack Attack" pounce on his enemies that would reveal him to be just that—to the realization that his style is better described as "No Drama Obama," seemingly pursuing goals the way a professional politician should.

Today, a new beginning starts, and a new road awaits; not an easy one, but a path guided by different hopes and expectations, with a common core belief that changing the course is necessary. Very quickly we will realize the different, conflicting visions of hope, the different roads and priorities for change, and the various voices clamoring recognition. That is when Senator Obama's true mettle will be tested. In his capacity to inspire and lead all these divergent forces, as well as to bridge and coalesce them, lies his potential as a great President—and his greatest potential to fail if he does not do so. Congratulations Senator Obama. Congratulations America.

What Now, Senator McCain?

November 22, 2008

In the closing days of the election, Senator Obama held several rallies in Florida. After one of the final ones, in Jacksonville, he held an interview with Rachel Maddow, from *MSNBC* and *Air America Radio*. Within this interview, Ms. Maddow asked why was the Obama campaign not attacking Senator McCain more intensely, when the opposing camp was slinging mud left and right, directly from the campaign committee, from the RNC and through PACs? The answer was as prescient as disarming: "Rachel, in case you haven't noticed, we are winning; and I am going to have to govern with these folks." True to his word, shortly after the election President Elect Obama met with Senator McCain, in a highly visible symbol of his attempt to be the president "of all of the United States."[5]

The role of Senator McCain does not seem as clear now, mostly because of his own transformation within the campaign. He may hopefully return to his "maverick" ways and truly stand by principle, now that he is no longer pressured by Rovian campaign handlers. He may now lead an opposition based on governmental policy and issue differences, not on political posturing. If anything, with the election of Senator Obama the American electorate sent a message to Atwater/Rovian political strategists regarding the wedge issues and polarizing tactics used for political posturing.

But in a—perhaps unintended—consequence of this Republican Party defeat, it seems that only the most polarized of counties remained Republican. With Senator Obama taking independents, moderates and centrists away from the Republicans, moderate Republican candidates lost their seats, leaving the ones with more partisan and radical agendas in place. This is more obvious in the House, where there is a full election, as opposed to the Senate where only a third gets elected every two years. So, while Senator McCain says that "obviously" he is going to work to get along with the new administration, and all eyes are on the filibuster-proof majority of the Senate, the House is in danger of becoming a battlefield of ideological divisiveness, with a Democratic majority in danger of bullying an increasingly bitter Republican minority into submission.

That the Republican Party is in disarray and needs rebuilding is obvious. The country requires a loyal opposition, bent on the true principle of "country first," not as a campaign or partisan slogan. Senator McCain's role here seems also obvious, yet tough. His influence in the shaping of the party is not diminished, as he is its nominal leader; but will have to cede soon to others—he lost the election, after all. The leadership of the Republican Party has to recognize that conducting a campaign focused on energizing the base did not work, as only in the Appalachian belt did Republican votes increase over the 2006 and 2004 elections. All other regions of the country had more people, by percentage, vote Democratic than in the previous election (*New York Times* 2008). Not only that, voter abstention among the Republican demographic seems to have run high in key swing states, such as Ohio and Pennsylvania, perhaps turned off by the extreme attacks and rhetoric with no obvious substance on the one hand, perhaps turned off by a tinge of racism on the other, maybe simply disenchanted—which is a potential strategy from either party, trying to drive down turnout of voters from the opposing party.

According to exit polls, it is significant that Senator Obama had more men overall voting for him than did Senator McCain (historically, the percentage of men voting Republican is greater than those voting Democrat), though more white men voted for McCain. It is probable that that means that absenteeism among white men was pronounced, in all economic groups but the 50-75K strata. (*New York Times* 2008)

Thus, the key question for McCain and the Republicans is: did these voters stay home because they saw in McCain a type of Republican (moderate) they did not like? Or did they not vote because of the disgust over the wedge politicking that characterized the McCain-Palin ticket towards the end? And, how did Governor Palin affect the ticket? Where they afraid of a Sarah Palin vice presidency? Or, furthermore, of a Sarah Palin presidency? (not so out of question after all). In any case, these were Republicans that did not want to vote for either McCain or Obama. It is in the answer to those questions that Republicans must come to terms with who they are and how they can establish a loyal opposition, an opposition that does not divide the country, but unites it, respecting diversity and not demonizing ideology, maintaining the idea of *E Pluribus, Unum,* (From Many, One), which is a tenet of our founding fathers' wisdom. This is where Senator McCain will find his role and true test, as it is not yet his time to fade away.

Notes

1.   Estimated by Dr. Michael McDonald, of the Department of Public and International Affairs at George Mason University, to be 131.2 million votes cast, or a 61.6 percent turnout (McDonald 2008).
2.   Obviously, in many cases, Republicans also inserted wedge issues in the ballots to motivate their partisans to vote. In the case of California, for example, it may be that some Democratic voters did not think they would make a difference in Senator Obama's chances to win the State if they voted for him and thus did not go vote, or simply were indifferent to ballot propositions. Possibly this was a factor in the victory of Proposition 8, the "Ban Gay Marriage" proposition, for which 52.2 percent voted for: 6,838,107 votes out of 13,084, 570. In the presidential race 60.9 percent voted for Senator Obama, 8,063,473 votes out of 13,213,832 cast for this ballot line (Bowen 2008). This proposition is expected to be ruled unconstitutional, as majorities cannot impose their will over minorities in order to ban legal rights that the majority freely enjoys, forfeiting the principle of equal protection under the law (Fourteenth Amendment to the Constitution of the United States).
3.   Dr. Michael McDonald analyzes voter turnout in his ongoing *United States Election Project.* He categorizes voters by voting-age population, the common demographic measure used as the divisor when determining turnout and defined as all residents eighteen or older, and voter-eligible population, his best estimate of people eligible to vote, which excludes felons, parolees, and non-citizen residents. The final numbers for Senator Obama, using Dr. McDonald's calculations and definitions, after all votes were counted were 50.95 percent of votes cast, 31.4 percent of voting-eligible population, and 28.9 percent of all citizens of voting age. In using the same set of data, George W. Bush's numbers for 2000 are 47.88 percent of votes cast, 25.96 for voting-eligible population, and 23.94 percent of voting-age population. For 2004 his numbers were 50.73 percent, 30.49 percent, and 28.10 percent respectively (McDonald 2008).
4.   Senator McCain's concession speech consisted of three parts: acknowledgment of defeat, acknowledgment of his supporters, and call for conciliation. While the third part is what has been called "gracious and bipartisan" the first part suggested that it was the African American vote that had propelled the victory for Senator Obama: "In a contest as long and difficult as this campaign has been, his success alone commands my respect for his ability and perseverance. But that he managed to do so by inspiring the hopes of so many millions of Americans who had once wrongly believed that they had little at stake or little influence in the election of an

American president is something I deeply admire and commend him for achieving. This is an historic election, and I recognize the special significance it has for African Americans and for the special pride that must be theirs tonight." In my view, a gracious acknowledgement of defeat without an attempt at divisiveness would have been to state how proud all Americans—not just African Americans—should feel about Barack Obama's election.

5.   In an amusing anecdote that illustrates the entrenched cynicism of the American political environment, a Republican Congresswoman from Florida, Ileana Ross-Lehtinen, hung up twice on President Elect Obama's call on her to congratulate her on her reelection and to offer to work together in the Foreign Relations Committee, of which she is part. She thought the calls were pranks from a local radio station and later said, "Why would Obama want to call a little slug like me?" After realizing the misunderstanding, she of course talked with the president elect, and they shared a laugh over the issue (Clark 2008).

Conclusions

In Transition

November 25, 2008

Barack Obama has been clear on this point over and over again: There is only one president of the U.S. at the time. In spite of that, the accelerated pace of events in our modern world and the high profile related to his election make all of his actions within the interregnum, market- and policy-affecting changers. At this point, in the middle of an economic crisis of unprecedented magnitude in modern times, the faltering leadership coming from the Bush administration has left a vacuum being filled by the incoming administration's presence, statements, and expectations. These actions have led to a direct effect on the markets and on the confidence of the country, to the extent that some commentators have called this transition period, a "split screen presidency"

That carefully chosen "deliberate haste" oxymoron is in full throttle within the president elect's executive team choosing the next government's members. It also would seem that they are reaching out to seasoned political, policy and technocrat experts to bolster the president elect's own capabilities. The charge that he is farming from Clinton bureaucracies and thus not bringing "change" is relatively unfounded because, after all, the Clinton administration was the last Democratic-led administration. Any pool of governmental executive experience will include a large number of former Clinton officials, obviously, and it is in the choices actually made that we may see what the new president's policies will be like.[1]

His visible outreach to current administration officials, including President Bush, is a signal to Republican Party members and sympathizers that he will probably be also reaching to within that party's ranks to bolster his own team. This would include the ideas that John Kerry was presenting on the last *Meet the Press* before the election (on November 2), in particular the ones referring to Congress:

Now, as to the management of the Congress, my advice, if it was asked for—and I, certainly, as a senator will weigh in—is that we don't need to pass things by 51 votes or 60 votes. We need to build 85-vote majorities. And I am confident—everything about Barack Obama's campaign has been inclusivity, has been reaching across the aisle.... He is going to govern in a way that brings the country together, and no matter what our majority, he's going to seek to reach a broader consensus because that's the only way we can govern America at this time. (Kerry 2008)

The hard part of bipartisan outreach will be to drive home policies seemingly contradictory to what some partisan Republicans claim are the tenets of their party, in particular as it refers to fiscal responsibility. There is a major economic crisis, and that is obvious. A revival—or revision—of Keynesian principles[2] is probable, requiring an astonishing increase in deficit spending in order to give that true economic "jolt" Mr. Obama referred to on November 24 and some Republican lawmakers will be grandstanding in the name of principles that the Republican administration has not kept over the last eight years.[3]

Although somewhat revised Keynesian policies could be in the offing, simple deficit spending is not a clear answer to the economic "cratering" we are faced with. If that were the case, we would be in boom times right now! The appeal of Senator Obama's message and the team he seems to be gathering is the expectation that he will identify correctly where and how to direct public spending to improve the core of the economy: the manufacturing base, the infrastructure, public health, and the welfare of the middle class. Deficit spending on its own does not a *new deal* make, as we burn dollars in the desert to no avail, and we increase the deficit and national debt to record levels, all the while lowering the standard of living for most Americans. A true structural change, placing Keynesianism over Monetarism, may be coming. We will be talking about "Obama Republicans" for some time to come, as these policies offer in the mid and long term more fiscal responsibility than the debt neutrality and natural business cycle principles that characterized Reaganomics (i.e., "unmanageable" market forces).

It is unfortunate that the Republican Party has moved away from conservative principles of individualism, fiscal responsibility and governmental non-intrusion, and that it has been hijacked by extremists seeking polarization in the use of power to force political agendas, using spend-and-borrow policies for populist pandering. We do need a loyal opposition that is dedicated to the ideals of the Union and Country, seeking common solutions within the boundaries of civilized discourse and dialogue. The opposition is not there to "check" the power of the ruling party. The opposition is a control mechanism that allows concerted movement towards the welfare of our social and our political state, not to wield a paralyzing gridlock tool.

The Obama era is not clearly defined, and could yet be a fiasco. Many pitfalls lay ahead including: The potential mandate and majorities in congress that the election seemingly delivered, and resulting in high expectations of quick change; the weakness of clear conservative thought that used to be entrusted to Republicans, which endangers the balance brought by constructive dialogue in government; and internal rivalries driven by the ambition of factions within an emboldened Democratic majority.

Given President Elect Obama's demonstrated penchant for control, moderation, reflection, and expert consultation, it should not be expected that external factors such as the economy or geopolitical issues will in fact be the ones that threaten the core of his presidency. It is the ability with which he navigates the new political landscape that will prove his most treacherous challenge. Our country is at a crossroads wherein he has the opportunity to redefine the role of government in American society, just as Reagan did and FDR did. Only time will tell if he succeeds. Will we all be better off? It is our hope.

An Innovation Imperative

December 6, 2008

Consolidation, restructuring and organizational reengineering can take an existing company or group of companies just so far, as it is only within newly entrepreneurially driven technological change and renewal that true competitive industry emerges. This is the core of Schumpeter's (1942) creative destruction concept that resurfaces from time to time, with each cycle of innovation bringing displacement and pain to our labor markets and industries. It is however within this process that true capitalist renewal occurs.

Government intervention may channel and stimulate or, misapplied, stifle and hinder the required changes needed to revolutionize the existing technological base. Changes are required in order to protect our social fabric, and make our industry competitive worldwide. But, the required changes are such a hard call when referring to the particulars! Is the automotive industry's malaise particular to it or generic to all manufacturing in America? The structural deficiencies of our manufacturing models have been around for a long time, allowing other countries to overcome the U.S. in many fields, including auto manufacturing (Toyota anyone?). And, if protecting obsolescing products and technologies were policy, we would still be mostly using typewriters and would continue using instamatic and Polaroid cameras forever.[3]

It is possible that, by taking a hard look to the way in which we approach financial reporting and expectations for all companies, we could find a major root of the problem. Our economy will have a hard time turning around until the focus that favors increasing quarterly profits and rising dividends, over long term investment and capital reserves, shifts. By no coincidence, General Motors' top layers of operational management have mostly come from their own financial executive ranks (Forbes 2008). GM is the one out of the three auto giants that is deemed at this time to have the greatest aversion to innovation, having stifled Saturn, dumped the EV1 (electric vehicle), as well as stopped development of the mini-van, over perceived short term financial negatives (Bunkley 2006, Maynard 2008).

At this moment, however, it is important to devise a safety net and transition for the displaced workers that have resulted from the consequences of everyone's financial short term gain focus, as opposed to envisioning strategic practices of saving and investment in real assets. Practices that should have been expected from an industry requiring long term investments, long development lead times, and deployment of capital outlays over extended periods of time.

The technological and manufacturing base of our country cannot nonchalantly dismiss the churning of businesses and jobs without the social consequences we are facing now.[4] These include increased social displacement and maladjustment, and increased income distribution inequalities. Over the last few years, the increase in productivity by the job force has not been reflected in an increase in compensation, decreasing job creation yet increasing wealth inequality (see chapter 3, note 1 and Oliner & Sichel 2008).

With the major manufacturing sectors using cheap oil and gasoline as their primary energy source and technological foundation, the increased dependency of our whole economy on these traditional sources becomes a threat, but, could it be an opportunity as well? If the threat is used to stimulate a technological base shifting that generates new independent industries and creates new jobs and spurs new businesses then it could become an opportunity at the same time.

From my perspective, having lived during a third of my life in a country run by oil money, I have seen the consequences of oil overdependence. The illusion of abundant resources created by a government's subsidized energy, national fund transfer policies and interventionism leads to overdependence on the "oil energy fix," a stagnant industrial sector, and an artificial standard of living with social mobility based on political control and affiliation—which becomes the new source for financial resources—with the consequent social and political turbulence.[5]

The high volatility of oil prices comes from its mutual interdependence on the growth of the world economies. When expectations of growth are low or negative, oil prices decrease—and they can decrease substantially, as we have seen. The record high prices during the early summer of 2008 were probably—and reportedly—based on the same type of speculative behavior that also caused the artificial pricing of real estate securitized instruments and eventually reverted into the global financial crisis in September and the subsequent meltdown. With the bursting of the financial and commodity speculation bubbles, as well as with the expectation of serious alternate energy initiatives, the price of oil spiraled down, starting when Al Gore announced the Decade to Energy Independence challenge (Broder 2008). But the temporary illusion of cheap energy created by currently low oil prices is pernicious to society, perpetuating the cycle of ever increasing dependence on this scarce commodity.

It is in America's best interests to shift away from a technological base predicated on low priced oil-dependent energy, and to enable a manufacturing platform based on multiple sources of energy. This, in turn, will decrease the speculative volatility of energy prices. The next wave of manufacturing technologies and innovations would then, most likely, be focused on a more efficient use of resources and on the generation and distribution of energy. This technological paradigm shift may bring such things as energy net-generating homes on reversible distribution lines, as opposed to net-consuming ones;[6] a new infrastructure for fueling vehicles; new urban transportation modes; new container, recycling, and biodegradable technologies; and different and effective uses of existing hydrocarbon resources such as oil and natural gas. The transition to this technological base will result in a manufacturing base displacement and economic factor dislocation; however, if a social net is in place, it could be managed with a view towards safeguarding the people affected by such displacement and dislocation.

This brings us back to the example at hand. Should we let the auto industry sink? Maybe, but surely we must not let it crash. It may be in its sinking that a new future and renewed auto industry emerges, perhaps devoid of manipulated quarterly expectations and with a greater focus on the long term. But for every worker currently affected we must have an answer to the questions: *"What now? How do I make ends meet this month?"* Hard questions to answer but questions that go hand in hand with deciding on the auto industry bailout and, for that matter, when deciding the future of our whole manufacturing base.[7] The impact of government supports on the industry, if not carefully crafted, may have international trade consequences, including potential WTO sanctions. That is why the transformational nature of the supports, focused on technological change, as well as the requirement of payback by the automakers, is critical to maintain the industry competitive worldwide.

It is the role of our representatives in Congress, in concert with the sometimes mentioned cabinet level office of technology and management innovation, to stimulate as well as to balance the required painful restructuring of our manufacturing base, with the capacity to create a safety net that allows the transition of our workforce to that new manufacturing base. And, even though it sounds lofty, we must remember that this transition is about people that have invested years upon years in obsolescing technological platforms, people that will be unable to be placed in new industries easily, or at all. As the baby boom echo generation enters the workforce, older baby boomers will find it harder and harder to find a place in the labor market. We are on the threshold of a social catastrophe for this aging generation, which face little hope of meaningful retirement. It is in the balancing of the social net and the capacity for technological innovation that the difficult task of our Congress lays.

A More Perfect Government: A Delivering of Expectations

December 23, 2008

Hope is an interesting word; a good one for a beginning, and a good one for an end. The Obama Campaign of 2008 was nearly flawless, resulting in a president elected with a clear majority of the votes cast, elected by more than just a single electoral swing state, winning states in both coasts, the south, the rust belt and the west, and with no butterfly ballot doubts, long recount battles, or waiting on judges' decisions for the results. President elect Obama's coattails have increased the majorities of Democrats in both houses and raised the expectations of his supporters that see in him the possibility of a renewal of the American dream. Out of these expectations of renewal the pent-up agendas of many stakeholders will tug and pull on the new president, seeking great change in a brief moment, in a rush to keep the moment from passing. Many will call to speed up on campaign promises and may be quick to jump and react to perceived breaches of these promises.[8] Others have already signaled a readiness to challenge aggressively these agendas—as well as the new president himself—possibly out of fear, maybe out of self-interest, probably with sincerity.

It is the effective professional politician the one that gathers coalitions around his or her adopted positions on the issues, and uses these coalitions to formulate policies that enable these positions. It seems that Barack Obama is an effective politician in that regard, as his campaign operation was based on this praxis, and it raised the expectations of voters from all regions and political sides. Expectations that he would be able to use his skills to rapidly transform the way the country is led, and lead the charge into a better future. Expectations reiterated by Obama's rally cry calling "fire it up, ready to go!"[9] and multiplied by the results of a well run campaign.

His capacity to inspire and deliver results during the campaign leads many to believe he can do the same from the seat of government. He may have the skill to do so but, as he himself already suggested, there are many difficulties ahead. His first test of leadership requires a Churchill, FDR, or John F. Kennedy sacrifice sound bite moment of *"Nothing to offer but blood, sweat and tears"* or *"Nothing to fear but fear itself"* or *"Ask not what your country can do for you..."* shortly after inauguration or at the inauguration itself to launch his presidency; an inspiring line wrought to temper expectations while calling for action.

The management of these expectations may create one of President Obama's greatest challenges. He ran as the candidate of hope and of change, and these are fickle ideals upon which to sustain a presidency. In transforming these ideals into an operational reality, a reality that faces political resistance from multiple fronts, a frail economy with structural flaws, and an internationally isolated United States, we can only hope that President Obama can truly shed the ballast from the past and propel our country into the new millennium.

And, as the Obama era begins, I expect he will deliver on the hope.

Notes

1.   By the same token, ratifying Robert Gates as secretary of defense is almost logical. The nation is at war in two different areas of the world, and to restructure the whole chain of command at this time may be unwise. Mr. Gates now has a new commander in chief, with new and seemingly clear priorities and objectives. Mr. Gates is in the best position to ensure that the priorities of the new CIC are carried out most effectively and quickly.

2.   Primarily, Keynesian principles are based on the expectation that government led expansionary fiscal policies affect economic output, that is, government spending will affect the GDP positively. It would be revisionist to argue that tax cuts are

equal to government outlays. This idea is suspiciously close to the idea of debt neutrality, which has driven up the deficit, while not expanding output.

3. For example, despite all the union concessions and government protections over the years, the steel manufacturing industry in the U.S. has been transformed by the shift in technologies. The advent of the mini-mills created such a radical change in the way the industry was structured that, for example, U.S. Steel (founded in 1901) went from employing almost 350,000 people in 1943 to less than 30,000 in the year 2007. In 2007, US Steel produced 21.5 million metric tons of steel, ranking tenth in the world, and Nucor (an early pioneer of mini-mill technology in the U.S., and which opened its first mill in 1968), produced 20 MTons and ranked twelfth in the world, with only 18,000 employees. By contrast, Nippon Steel Corporation, (consolidated in 1970) ranked second in the world with 37.5 MTons of production in 2007 (World Steel Association 2008); in 2008 it had about 15,000 employees (Hoovers 2008).

4. According to Michael Porter, restructuring destroys about 30 million jobs a year (Porter 2008).

5. In 1976 Juan Pablo Perez Alfonzo, a Venezuelan politician that conceived and led the creation of OPEC, coined the term "Devil's excrement" when describing oil in his famous book, referring to the social and economic impact that overdependence on oil revenues had on society (Perez Alfonzo 1976, Useem 2003). Perhaps the overdependence by the U.S. and other industrialized or rapidly industrializing nations can be seen as a corollary of the economic concept of Dutch Disease—the impact on manufacturing sectors and moral fallout derived by the easy availability of a productive resource, and the high equivalent rents derived from such resource. Further research is required.

6. Energy conservation with a financial incentive: if a home can generate a portion of its energy needs with solar panels, for example, can conserve energy through the use of heat sinks, better insulation and behavioral practices, and can sell off some of its excess energy produced through reverse distribution lines, more people would in fact conserve energy.

7. To place the size of these so-called automotive industry "bailout" packages in perspective, the Chrysler loan guarantees of 1979 were $1.2 billion, and the 1990's S&L rescue ultimately cost around $150 billion. The TARP has a spending authority of $700 billion to "rescue" the financial sector, while the auto industry proposed package is approximately $15 billion. President Bush finally using executive authority, used funds from the TARP to provide financial assistance to the automakers. The final figure was $17 billion.

8. As an example, the adverse reaction by gay and lesbian advocacy groups to naming the Rev. Rick Warren to lead the invocation at the inaugural ceremonies.

9. His summoning mantra at the end of his final primary season rally in Mitchell, SD on June 1 and before heading to St. Paul on June 3, the date when the number of delegates won in the primaries sealed his nomination.

Appendix 1

Electoral College Graphs 2008

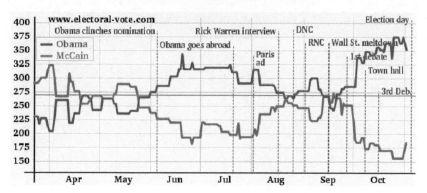

The graph above shows the number of electoral votes for each candidate since March 22. The horizontal line shows the 270 electoral vote mark needed to be elected president. The vertical lines show the boundaries between the months. The next graph shows the electoral votes again but omits the "barely commited" states. The electoral votes of a state only count in this graph if the candidate has a margin of 5 percent or more over his opponent.

Source: electoral-vote.com (November 1, 2008)

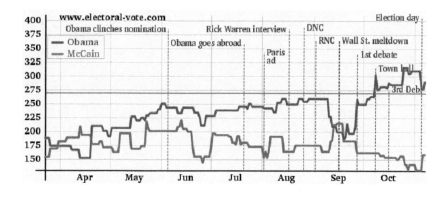

Appendix 2

Voters and Non-Voters—Who are They?

The Census Bureau report allows us to answer the questions of who votes, who does not, who is registered and who is not from a statistical point of view, perhaps reinforcing stereotypes, but also shaking some of them. The information currently available (Holder 2006) corresponds to the 2004 census. A new report comes out in 2010, which will be interesting to contrast with the available numbers for voters and non-voters.

- *Person most likely to vote:* A person within a family with income greater than $100,000, a homeowner for more than five years in the west of the country, married, between forty-five and seventy-four years of age, a veteran with a bachelor's degree up to an advanced degree. Also tends to be white non-Hispanic, employed, and a woman, possibly from the northeast.
- *Person least likely to vote:* A person with less than a high school degree, with a family income of less than $20,000, and someone who is separated from their wife or husband. Probably, this person is also unemployed, Hispanic, and younger than twenty-five years of age.
- *Person not registered to vote:* Regarding registrations, those who are most likely to not be registered to vote are Asian or Hispanic, renters, and those without a high school degree—but this includes a portion of the population still in high school. Non registered voters may also have a family income less than $30,000, have been living in their current residence for less than a year, most likely in the west, are younger than twenty-four years old, possibly black, and could be unemployed.
- *Reasons not to register:* Regarding reasons not to register, the prevalent reason was "not interested in the election or not involved in politics" (46.6 percent). This is followed by "did not meet registration deadlines" (17.4 percent), and an additional group that said they "did not know where to register," (4.5 percent) making a combined 21.9 percent of people who perhaps wanted to vote but could not register for lack of adequate and timely information. If we added to these categories the 3.7 percent that are skeptics who think voting makes no difference, election results can be impacted by raising voter consciousness and providing adequate registration information. 72.2 percent (46.6+21.9+3.7) of the people not registered to vote can be affected by these registration and education programs.

- *Reasons for not voting:* In the top of the list among the reasons for not voting were "too busy/conflicting schedule" or "out of town" with close to 30 percent combined, and "illness or disability" which, when combined with "inconvenient polling place" and "transportation problems" accounted for 20.5 percent of non voters. "Registration problems" (6.8 percent of people who did not vote), typically associated with voter disenfranchisement—people who went to vote but were turned away—was the greatest among Hispanics that had recently moved; blacks had, as a percentage, greater "transportation problems."

Bibliography

Alexander, Gregory S. "Interpreting Legal Constructivism," Book review of *Reconstructing American Law* by Bruce A. Ackerman, Harvard University Press, 1984 in *Cornell Law Review*, Vol. 71:249, 1985-1986.

Andron, Scott. "The CPI May Be Right, Believe It or Not." *Miami Herald*, June 23 2008.

Associated Press Wire Service. "Russian Defense Budget may Rise 25% in 2009," *USA Today*, September 19, 2008.

Bachelet, Pablo. "U.S. 'Concerned' about FARC Uranium." *Miami Herald*, March 28, 2008.

Bachmann, Michele. Interview with Chris Matthews, *MSNBC. Hardball*, October 17, 2008.

Barbaro, Michael. "As a Director, Clinton Moved Wal-Mart Board, but Only So Far," *New York Times*, May 20, 2007.

Barrionuevo, Alexei. "Strong Economy Propels Brazil to World Stage," *New York Times*, July 31, 2008.

BBC News. "Rumsfeld 'Wanted Cheap War,'" *BBC News*, March 30, 2003.

Becker, Jo and Don Van Natta Jr. "For McCain and Team, a Host of Ties to Gambling," *New York Times*, September 27, 2008.

Bernton, Hal and David Heath. "Palin's Earmark Requests: More per Person than any Other State." *Seattle Times*, September 2, 2008.

Bowen, Debra. California General Election, Presidential Election Certified Results, Tuesday November 4, 2008.

Broder, John M. "Gore Urges Change to Dodge an Energy Crisis," *New York Times*, July 18, 2008.

Bunkley, Nick. "G.M. Cancels Plan for Saturn Minivan," *New York Times*, November 22, 2006.

Bureau of Labor Statistics. US Department of Labor, Information retrieval system at www.bls.gov – Archived News Releases for Real Wages. 2008.

Burman, Len , S. Khitatrakun, G. Leiserson, J. Rohaly, E. Toder, and B. Williams. "An Updated Analysis of the 2008 Presidential Candidates' Tax Plans," Tax Policy Center at the Urban Institute and Brookings Institution, August 15 2008.

Bush, George W. "Address to a Joint Session of Congress and the American People," *The White House, News & Policies* at www.whitehouse.gov, September 20 2001.

Magnusson, Paul, Andy Reinhardt. Seanna Browder and bureau reports. "China: The Great Brawl - U.S. Companies Battle a New, Vigorous Threat to Beijing's Trade Status," *Business Week,* June 16 1997.

Carl, Tracy and Dan Keane. "Bolivia to Nationalize Mining Industry," *Washington Post*, January 10, 2007.

Cassreino, Terry. "Corrected calculation shows Obama with 20 Mississippi delegates and Clinton with 13," *Mississippi Democratic Party News Release*, April 4, 2008.

China Daily News. "US Senators Act to Repeal China PNTR Status," *China Daily News*, February 10, 2006.

Clark, Cammy. "Oops! South Florida Lawmaker, Suspecting a Prank, Hangs up on Obama," *Miami Herald,* December 4 2008.

CNN Money. "Flu Toll on Economy Mounts," October 16, 2003.

CNN. "'You Are Either With Us or Against Us,'" In report on visit and joint news conference by President Bush and France President Jacques Chirac. November 6, 2001.

Collins, S. R., Kriss, J. L., Doty, M. M. and S. D. Rustgi. "Losing Ground: How the Loss of Adequate Health Insurance Is Burdening Working Families: Findings from the Commonwealth Fund Biennial Health Insurance Surveys, 2001–2007," *The Commonwealth Fund,* August, 2008.

DeMocker, Judy. "Connect With Far-Off Grandchildren." Grandparents.com. 2008.

Depalma, Anthony. "Mother Denies Abuse of Son Suing to End Parental Tie," *New York Times*, September 25, 1992.

Dionne, E. J. "A Catholic Shift to Obama?" *Washington Post*, October 21, 2008.

Ellingwood, Ken. "Mexico vs. Drug Gangs: A Deadly Clash for Control," *Los Angeles Times*, June 3, 2008.

Energy Information Administration. "US Imports by Country of Origin (2002-2007) – Crude Oil."

Feller, Ben. "Bush Wishes Obama Well on a 'Great Journey,'" *USA Today*, November 5 2008.

Fishman, Charles. "The Wal-Mart You Don't Know." *Fast Company*, No. 77, December, 2003.

Forbes. Forbes Profiles of Corporate Executives, 2008.

Fredrix, Emily. "Tough Economy Demands Spam - Sales of the Pork Concoction Climb as Living Costs Rise", Associated Press, as published in *San Francisco Chronicle*, May 29, 2008.

Freire, Paulo. *Letters to Cristina*, translated by Donaldo Pereira Macedo. New York/London: Routledge, 1996.

Fritze, John. "Palin did not Ban Books in Wasilla as Mayor," *USA Today*, September 10, 2008.

Fuller, R. Buckminster. *Operating Manual for Spaceship Earth*. Champaign: S. Illinois University Press, 1969.

Fung, K. C., Hitomi Iizaka and Alan Siu. "The Giant Sucking Sound: Is China Diverting Foreign Direct Investment from East Asia and Latin America?" *Economic Forum*, January-February 2005, Hong Kong Trade Development Council.

Goodwin, N., J. A. Nelson, F. Ackerman and T. Weisskopf, lead authors; C. J. Cleveland Topic Editor. "Distribution of Wealth," in *Encyclopedia of Earth*. Content Partner: Global Development and Environment Institute, 2007.

Gordon, Greg. "Furor Over ACORN Allegations Gaining Momentum," *Miami Herald*, October 24, 2008.

Hall, Robert. VP and International Trade Counsel of the National Retail Federation in testimony before the Subcommittee on Trade of the House Committee on Ways and Means Hearing on U.S.-China Trade Relations and Renewal of China's Most-Favored-Nation Status, June 17, 1997.

Halloran, Liz. "McCain Suspends Campaign, Shocks Republicans," *US News & World Report*, September 24, 2008.

Hernandez, Sandra. "TIPS Flunk Inflation Test as Fuel, Food Overtake CPI." *Bloomberg,* July 7, 2008.

Holder, Kelly. "Voting and Registration in the Election of November 2004— Population Characteristics." *U.S. Census Bureau*, Pub P20-556, issued March 2006.

Hoovers. Business Reports, 2008. Dun & Bradstreet.

Horowitz, Jason. "Senator Clinton, 2001-2008: Smart, Hardworking, Unextraordinary." *New York Observer*, December 8, 2008.

Jisi, Wang, Nicholas Lardy and Robert C. Berring "China After MFN," *Contemporary East Asia*, Number 2, October 1994. Institute of East Asian Studies, a unit of the International and Area Studies at the University of California, Berkeley.

Kandilov, Ivan T. "Trade and Wages Revisited: The Effect of the China's MFN Status on the Skill Premium in U.S. Manufacturing." November 2008 (draft), North Carolina State University.

Kerry, John. *Meet the Press* interview, November 2, 2008. Transcript available at http://www.msnbc.msn.com/id/27502133.

Kmiec, Douglas W. "I'm Catholic and pro-Obama," *Miami Herald*, October 20 2008.

Knowlton, Brian. "Republican Says Bush Panders to the 'Agents of Intolerance': McCain Takes Aim At Religious Right," *International Herald Tribune*, February 29, 2000.

Liasson, Mara. "Clinton Makes a Play for Florida's Democrats," *NPR: All Things Considered*, January 28, 2008.

Lilly, Scott. "Sarah Palin, John McCain, and Earmarks." *Center for American Progress Fund*, September 4, 2008. http://www.americanprogressaction.org/issues/2008/palin_earmarks.html.

Los Angeles Times. "Mexico Under Siege: The Drug War at our Doorstep." *Los Angeles Times,* Continuing series 2007/09. Bylines by: Bartletti, D., Bonello, D., Bustillo, M., Dickerson, M., Ellingwood, K., Larrubia, E., Marosi, R., Meyer, J., Pringle, P., Quinones, S., Ranoa, R., Sanchez, C., Schmitt, R., Serrano, R., Wilkinson, T., and reports by *Times* staff and the Associated Press.

Markowitz, Arthur. "GATT, MFN Approval Deadlines Loom - General Agreement on Tariffs and Trade, Most Favored Nation - Free Trade Forum," *Discount Store News*, May 16, 1994.

Maynard, Micheline. "At G.M., Innovation Sacrificed to Profits," *New York Times*, December 5, 2008.

McDonald, Michael. United States Election Project (ongoing study). Department of Public and International Affairs, George Mason University, 2008.

Mcdonnell, Patrick J. "Quake Aid has Pro-Chavez Message," *Los Angeles Times*, August 21, 2007.

Mitchell, G. and D. Hill. "Friday Final (?) Tally of Newspaper Endorsements—Obama In Landslide, at 287-159," *Editor & Publisher*, November 7, 2008.

Nader, Ralph. *Meet the Press* interview. February 24, 2008. Transcript available at http://www.msnbc.msn.com/id/23319215.

Nagourney, Adam. "Democrats Take a Tough Line on Florida Primary," *New York Times*, August 26, 2007.

Naím, Moises. "The Free Trade Paradox." *Foreign Policy,* September/October, 2007.

NAVSEA DC Museum: USS Forrestal (CVA 59) – Damage Control Fire Protection and CBR-D (http://www.dcfp.navy.mil/mc/museum/FOR-RESTAL/Forrestal1.htm).

New York Times. "Election Results 2008, National Exit Polls Table," *New York Times*, November 5, 2008.

Nicholas, Peter and Noam N. Leavey. "Hillary Clinton's Schedules Shed Little Light on Work as First Lady," *Los Angeles Times,* March 20, 2008.

Nicholas, Peter. "New Registrations Favor Democrats," *Los Angeles Times*, October 6, 2008.

Noonan, Peggy. "Palin and Populism - The Downside of Appealing to Joe Six-Pack," *Wall Street Journal*, October 3, 2008.

Novosti, Ria. "Venezuelan President Chavez to arrive in Russia July 22," Press release dated July 10, 2008.

Obama, Barack. *Dreams from My Father: A Story of Race and Inheritance.* New York: Times Books, 1995.

Obama, Barack. *Dreams from My Father: A Story of Race and Inheritance.* New York: Crown/Three Rivers Press, 2004.

Obama, Barack. *The Audacity of Hope: Thoughts on Reclaiming the American Dream.* New York: Crown/Three Rivers Press, 2006.

Office of Management and Budget. Official budget figures, 2008. The White House at www.whitehouse.gov/omb.

Ohlemacher, Stephen. "How Average is Your State?" *Associated Press*, 2007.

Oliner, Stephen D. and Daniel E. Sichel. "Explaining a Productive Decade: An Update," Presentation at the *Symposium on the Outlook for Future Productivity Growth Federal Reserve Bank of San Francisco*, San Francisco, November 14, 2008.

Perez Alfonzo, Juan Pablo. *Hundiéndonos en el Excremento del Diablo.* Barquisimeto, Venezuela: Editorial Lisbona, Colección Venezuela Contemporánea, 1976.

Porter, Michael. "Why America Needs an Economic Strategy," *Business Week*, October 30, 2008.

Rangel, Carlos. *Marx y Los Socialismos Reales y Otros Ensayos*. Caracas: Monte Avila Ed., 1989.

Rangel, Carlos. *The Latin Americans: Their Love Hate Relationship with the United States*. New Brunswick, NJ: Transaction Publishers, 1987.

Rendell, Ed. *Meet the Press* interview, March 9 2008. Transcript available at http://www.snbc.msn.com/id/23546011.

Reuters (a). "Experts Optimistic New Flu Vaccine Can Help Businesses Keep Productivity Up," July 2, 2008.

Reuters (b). "Venezuela's Chavez Seeks Arms Deals in Russia," *International Herald Tribune*, July 21, 2008.

Roan, Shari. "The 30-Day Myth; Treating Addiction Effectively, Rehab Centers are Finding, is Truly a Matter of Time. The Longer the Stay, the Better Chance for Success," *Los Angeles Times*, November 10, 2008.

Rutenberg, Jim. "The Battle of Perception Still Wages on Television," *New York Times*, April 23, 2008.

Safire, William. "Essay: Blizzard of Lies," *New York Times*, January 8, 1996.

Safire, William. "Essay; Habitual Prevaricator," *New York Times*, October 23 2000.

Savage, Charlie. "Bush Challenges Hundreds of Laws - President Cites Powers of his Office," *Boston Globe*, April 30, 2006.

Schumacher-Matos, Edward. "Contribution to Clinton Campaign Weighed," *Miami Herald*, Oct 28, 2007.

Schumpeter, Joseph A. *Capitalism, Socialism and Democracy*. New York: Harper, 1975, originally published in 1942.

Scott, Anna. "Did Clinton break Democrats' No Florida Campaigning Pledge?" *Herald Tribune*, January 28, 2008.

Scott, Robert E. "The China Trade Toll: Widespread Wage Suppression, 2 Million Jobs lost in the U.S.," *Economic Policy Institute*, Briefing Paper no. 219, July 2008.

Scott, Robert E. "The High price of 'Free' Trade: NAFTA's Failure has Cost the United States Jobs Across the Nation," *Economic Policy Institute*, Briefing Paper no. 147, November 2003.

Shear, Michael D. "DNC Strips Florida of 2008 Delegates," *Washington Post*, August 26, 2007.

Simon, Herbert A. "Bounded Rationality and Organizational Learning," *Organization Science*, Vol. 2, No. 1, February 1991.

United Nations Development Programme. "Human Development Report 2007/2008 – Fighting Climate Change: Human Solidarity in a Divided World," 2007/2008.

U.S. Department of Justice. "Bureau of Justice Statistics Bulletin," Office of Justice Programs, Pub. NCJ 224280, December 2008.

Useem, Jerry. "The Devil's Excrement," *Fortune Magazine*, February 3, 2003.

Vartabedian, Ralph and Richard A. Serrano. "Mishaps Mark John McCain's Record as Naval Aviator," *Los Angeles Times*, October 6, 2008.

Vistesen, Claus. "Brazil Country Outlook," *Brazil Economy Watch*, Copenhagen July 2008.

Waldman, Steven and Dan Gildoff. "Different Worldviews for Obama, McCain Faithful." Beliefnet.com (http://www.beliefnet.com/News/Politics/2008/11/Beliefnet-Election-2008-Exit-Poll-Results.aspx?p=1).

Washington Times. "FARC's Uranium Likely a Scam," *Washington Times*, March 19, 2008.

White House Press Release. "Pathways to Prosperity in the Americas," *The White House*, News & Policies, September 24, 2008.

World Steel Association. "Top Steel Producers 2007." 2008. Available at http://www.worldsteel.org/?action=storypages&id=284.

Yardley, William. "Palin's Start in Alaska: Not Politics as Usual." *New York Times*, September 2 2008.

Index

137

For Product Safety Concerns and Information please contact our EU
representative GPSR@taylorandfrancis.com Taylor & Francis Verlag GmbH,
Kaufingerstraße 24, 80331 München, Germany

Batch number: 08153776

Printed by Printforce, the Netherlands